W9-CBR-140

WAR in the RING

WAR *in the* RING

Joe Louis, Max Schmeling, and
the Fight between America and Hitler

JOHN FLORIO AND OUISIE SHAPIRO

ROARING BROOK PRESS

New York

Published by Roaring Brook Press
Roaring Brook Press is a division of Holtzbrinck Publishing Holdings
Limited Partnership
175 Fifth Avenue, New York, NY 10010
mackids.com

Library of Congress Control Number: 2018956075
ISBN: 978-1-250-15574-0

Our books may be purchased in bulk for promotional, educational,
or business use. Please contact your local bookseller or the Macmillan
Corporate and Premium Sales Department at (800) 221-7945 ext. 5442 or
by email at MacmillanSpecialMarkets@macmillan.com.

First edition, 2019
Book design by Aram Kim
Printed in the United States of America by LSC Communications,
Harrisonburg, Virginia

1   3   5   7   9   10   8   6   4   2

CONTENTS

PROLOGUE

June 22, 1938

America's got the jitters. It's all over the news that German Chancellor Adolf Hitler's army has taken Austria without a fight and is threatening to conquer other countries in Eastern Europe. Hitler is spreading his hatred of Jews; his Nazi party is taking prisoners and herding them to concentration camps. The headlines are scary.

HITLER SEIZES CONTROL OF AUSTRIA

NAZI THREAT ADDS TO JEWS' FEARS

NAZI PERSECUTION CONTINUES

The United States wants no part of Germany, the Nazis, or a global war.

At ten o'clock, New York time, the eyes of the world turn to a boxing ring in Yankee Stadium. There, the heavyweight champion of the world, a twenty-four-year-old black American named Joe Louis, is about to defend his title against a thirty-two-year-old white German, Max Schmeling.

As the two fighters climb through the ropes, the overhead lights beaming down on them, men and women across the United States lean in to their radios, hanging on the outcome.

In Germany, it's the middle of the night, but millions of residents have their lights on and their radios tuned to the broadcast coming over the phone lines.

The bell rings.

Louis moves to the center of the ring, his gloves raised. Schmeling does the same. Each carries the weight of his country on his back.

Showdown at Yankee Stadium, June 22, 1938.

Eighty thousand fans in the stadium hold their breath.

Seventy million more press their ears to the radio.

This is it.

This is the war in the ring.

CHAPTER 1

1932: Joe's Violin

America was in the midst of the Great Depression. The stock market had crashed two years earlier, and the slowdown was so severe that even the banks couldn't survive. Nearly ten thousand were on their way to shutting down, taking with them the life savings of millions of Americans. Billions of dollars evaporated. Countless businesses collapsed. People waited in long lines for bread or sought out charity kitchens for soup. The poorest of the poor, having lost their homes along with their money, pitched tents in local parks and slept outside.

In Detroit, the home of the nation's car industry, seventeen-year-old Joe Louis Barrow was on his way to school, his hand-me-down clothes barely fitting his six-foot frame. Like virtually every kid in the neighborhood, Joe had nothing in his pockets. But unlike the others, he had a musical instrument under his arm.

"Here I was," Joe later said, "big as a light heavyweight,

After the stock market crash, Americans line up for free food.

going to Bronson Vocational School, carrying this little bit of a violin. You can imagine the kidding I had to take. I remember one time some guy called me a sissy when he saw me with the violin, and I broke it over his head."

Joe's friend Thurston McKinney was fighting his way through the amateur ranks as a lightweight boxer. He suggested that Joe ditch the violin and join him in the ring. After all, there was big money to be made in boxing, and not a penny to be had in playing a stringed instrument. Just look at the heavyweight champ, Jack Dempsey, Thurston said. He retired four years ago, and he's still

A young Joe Louis Barrow practices the violin.

loaded. Joe wasn't sold on the idea, mostly because he knew how hard his mother worked to pay for his violin lessons.

As a small boy growing up in Alabama, Joe had been a quiet kid. While his brothers and sisters were outside playing, or picking cotton on the family patch, he would wander down to the nearby swamp and hunt snakes.

Joe's parents, Lillie Reese and Munroe Barrow, were the children of former enslaved people and worked as sharecroppers outside the town of LaFayette. Joe was the seventh of eight children, living in a shack with a sagging roof and loose floorboards. "It looked like a good wind would have blown it down," he said years later.

The strain of supporting a large family with the back-breaking work of picking cotton day in and day out landed Munroe in a psychiatric hospital when Joe was just two. Lillie was left to raise the children by herself for a few years until she married Pat Brooks, a widower with eight children of his own.

Joe fed the chickens and the hogs, and when he was old enough, joined the rest of his family under the blazing sun in the fields, bent over at the waist, dragging a seventy-pound sack of cotton behind him. At night he went to bed complaining about having to sleep in the same bed with two of his brothers.

The Barrow-Brooks clan was no different from hundreds of thousands of other struggling black families in the South. Joe's family was accustomed to the hard life in Alabama, but they heard that better-paying jobs could be found in the bustling cities up north. And when word got out that the Ford Motor Company in Detroit was paying as much as $7 a day to work in its factories—more than twice what sharecropping paid—Pat figured it was worth a shot. How could things be any worse in Detroit than they were in Alabama? At least there would be electricity and indoor plumbing, two luxuries they'd never had in the South. And so by 1926, Joe and his family were settled in Detroit and Pat was working at Ford.

The Barrow-Brooks family was part of the Great Migration that saw more than a million-and-a-half African Americans leave the South and move north and west in search of jobs and safety from violent threats, most of them coming from white supremacist groups like the Ku Klux Klan. A second wave would follow twenty years later, taking more than five million African Americans with it.

Even in booming Detroit, however, all was not rosy for black residents. As African Americans poured into the city, its color line grew more restrictive, forcing blacks to live in certain neighborhoods. Joe's family found housing in Black Bottom, the east side neighborhood named by 18th-century French explorers for the rich, black soil that had once been farmland. Block after block was lined with shops, schools, churches, bars, and pool halls, and the area offered a thriving nightlife of musicians and entertainers. Many of the homes were tenements that had been built quickly to accommodate the mass influx of Southern blacks.

A few years after moving to Detroit, Pat was out of work, having lost his job at the Ford plant when the stock market crashed in October 1929. It was all he and Lillie could do to hold on to their tenement.

Joe's friend Thurston kept pushing the fight game. You're a big, strong guy, he told Joe. If you stick with it, you're sure to rake in more money than any fiddler would dream of earning. Besides, he said, "You got to have education to be a good one on the violin. You got to read notes." Thurston had a point: Joe had no interest in learning music, and it would take years before he could develop his skills. Joe figured that he could learn how to box now and, if he was good at it, earn some money to help his family buy groceries.

Joe went with Thurston to the Brewster recreation center. The minute he walked in and heard the pitter-patter of speed bags and smelled the liniment oil, he was hooked.

"I looked at the ring, the punching bag, pulleys, the exercise mat, and it was love at first sight," he said.

Boxing suited Joe's temperament. He'd never been much of a talker; he had a stutter and preferred to keep to himself. And that's how the boxers worked out. Alone. Plus, Joe was strong from all his odd jobs after school. He would haul fifty pounds of ice up two flights of stairs while his friend Freddie would stay downstairs watching the delivery horse and carriage. The work had made his shoulders, back, and thighs even more muscular.

Thurston suggested that Joe join the gym with the fifty cents his mother had given him for violin lessons. Joe didn't like the idea. To him, spending that money on anything other than the violin would be the same as lying. But the allure of boxing was too strong.

Joe wound up spending the money on boxing lessons—and he used the twenty-five cents he made scrubbing floors for his sister, Emmarell, to cover his dues at the rec center. Then he told his mother what she didn't want to hear: He was quitting school and taking a job at Briggs Manufacturing, the factory that made truck bodies for Ford. Within days, he was hard at work pushing two-hundred-pound truck bodies onto a conveyor belt. The metal shells were so heavy that Joe felt as if someone was knifing him in the back every time he loaded one—but the job paid $25 a week. Every week, he gave his paycheck to his mother to replace the money he'd misspent and help her run the house. And every day, after finishing work at five o'clock, he'd have a quick dinner at home before rushing out to the rec center.

One night, Joe got home from the gym around eleven, and Pat stopped him before he got to his bedroom.

Joe at the boxing gym.

"Where you been, Joe?" his stepfather asked.

"Over at the gym, working out."

"I thought so. Well, I'm warnin' you, Joe, if you keep on wasting your time down at that gym, and foolin' around with boxing, you're never gonna amount to nothing!"

Joe had a lot of respect for Pat—the man was taking any job he could find to raise his brood. But another friend at the gym, a more experienced boxer named Holman Williams, who'd been training Joe, gave his student a talking to.

"Joe," he said, pointing at his friend's large, powerful fists, "I think you've got what it takes."

Joe chose to listen to Holman over his stepfather, mostly because he liked what Holman said. Determined to prove Pat wrong, Joe quit his job and began spending his days and nights at the gym. Holman coached him on the basics of boxing: how to throw a jab, the straight left hand that keeps opponents away, and how to follow it with a right cross, the powerful punch that could knock them out. Joe quickly discovered there was so much more to boxing than punching. There was strategy. Sure, Joe was strong, but the trick was to use his strength to exploit his opponent's weaknesses.

In 1932, Joe fought an amateur match against Johnny Miler, a member of that year's U.S. Olympic team. Joe thought he would beat him easily, but Miler knocked him down seven times in two rounds. Joe kept getting up, trying to weather the storm, but Miler was the better fighter.

"I was a badly beaten and bruised boy when I slipped into the house that night," he said years later. "I didn't want anybody to see me, so I ducked upstairs."

Joe went to the gym the next day. "I tell you I was sore and aching, but my pride hurt more."

When he returned home that night, Pat sat him down and persuaded him to give up the idea of boxing for a living. Dutiful Joe found a job at Ford's River Rouge plant. Again, he was loading truck bodies onto a conveyor belt. But he'd soon had enough. "I couldn't take it anymore," he said. "I figured, if I'm going to hurt that much for twenty-five dollars a week, I might as well go back and try fighting again." So he left Ford and prepared for the 1933 amateur Golden Gloves competition.

Holman worked him even harder than before. Atler Ellis, the owner of the gym, noticed that Joe had a strong right hand but didn't use his left very well. Ellis tied Joe's right to the ring post and told Thurston McKinney to box Joe.

"Tie me loose," Joe yelled as Thurston wailed away with both hands, and Joe struggled to block the onslaught of punches using only his left.

The hard training began to pay off. Joe knocked out opponent after opponent and, in 1933, wound up winning Detroit's Golden Gloves competition.

Having dropped his last name, Barrow, Joe Louis was making a name for himself. One of his most enthusiastic supporters was John Roxborough, a small-time black racketeer who'd gotten rich buying and selling real estate, and even richer by running an illegal lottery. Roxborough viewed Joe as a diamond in the rough—a kid who could be molded into a champion. Roxborough offered the young fighter a management deal: Live in my house, dine on steaks and chops instead of hot dogs, and I'll give you $6 a week in pocket money. I'll even set you up with your own boxing gear. When you turn pro, you can pay me with 25 percent of your ring earnings.

Joe knew deals like this didn't come along every day, and he saw Roxborough as "well encased in dignity and legitimacy." He agreed to Roxborough's terms, and by the time the national amateur title fights came around in 1934, he was well fed, well rested, and ready to go. That year, he won both the national Golden Gloves and AAU championships as a light heavyweight, the category just below the prestigious heavyweight class.

It was obvious that Joe was ready for a higher level of competition, and Roxborough knew that representing him required a deeper knowledge of the fight game. Roxborough's first move was finding a comanager who'd be able to get Joe some professional fights. He partnered with the well-connected Chicago businessman Julian Black and together, they stood out as two of the first black managers in

Joe, a light heavyweight, with the 1934 Golden Gloves champions (second from right).

the sport. Roxborough then found Joe a trainer, another black man, ex-boxer Jack Blackburn.

The hard-drinking, bald-headed Blackburn weighed barely 135 pounds, but he had never walked away from a fight, be it in a ring or bar or on the street. He carried a souvenir from his violent past, a razor-deep scar running all the way from his left cheekbone to the corner of his bottom lip, and he had served nearly five years in prison for killing a man during an argument. Blackburn had been in more than a hundred pro bouts, many of them against far bigger opponents. When he hung up his gloves, he became a trainer, and by the time he met Joe, he had already turned several white boxers into champions. But he was reluctant to take Joe on because he knew that black heavyweights couldn't make it in the sport. The racism dividing America was rampant throughout society, and the world of boxing was no different.

Joe knew all about bigotry. He'd grown up in the Jim Crow South, where blacks were forced to live separate from whites. Blacks went to "colored" schools, lived in "colored" housing, and used "colored" facilities. Throughout the South, COLORED and WHITES ONLY signs were posted at train stations, bus depots, restaurants, parks and beaches, restrooms, and movie theaters. According to the 1896 Supreme Court case *Plessy v. Ferguson*, such division was legal as long as the facilities were "separate but equal." But the truth was that the black facilities, while separate, were anything but equal to their white counterparts.

The bigotry wasn't just unfair, it was violent. By the early 1920s, at least 1,200 African Americans were lynched in the South—that is, killed by white mobs in a frenzy of racist vigilante justice. The National Association for the Advancement of Colored People (NAACP) lobbied Congress to pass anti-lynching legislation called the Dyer Bill, but it was defeated in the Senate in 1922, and again in 1923 and 1924.

During the Great Depression, even as President Franklin Roosevelt created millions of jobs for unemployed Americans, blacks continued to suffer discrimination in the workplace and throughout all other aspects of society.

When black families took car trips throughout the South, they had to be aware of safe places to eat, sleep, and stop for gas. Since many establishments excluded them, black travelers packed food and extra gasoline in the car and, if there was room in the trunk, brought along portable toilets. They also knew to avoid certain communities after dark. These places were called sundown towns, and their residents went so far as to post billboards targeting African Americans that read, DON'T LET THE SUN GO DOWN ON YOU HERE. In other words, don't be seen in our town after dark.

As for boxing, the sport was controlled by white promoters—they were the ones who arranged the matches

Bus stations in the Jim Crow South separate black and white Americans.

and paid the boxers—and no whites wanted to see a black man become champion, whether in the South, the North, or anywhere else. Blackburn knew that Joe's talent didn't matter; white promoters would never give him a shot at the title. Blackburn himself had never gotten one, despite having been a top boxer in his day. Instead of earning big money, he'd fought in the back rooms of speakeasies, often paid with nothing more than a round of drinks. But when he saw the way Joe punched—when he witnessed the power in those brick-like fists—he changed his mind. This kid was worth it.

Cool as a Frozen Cucumber

In June 1934, Joe's team—Roxborough, Black, and Blackburn—decided it was time for their fighter to graduate out of the amateur ranks. As a professional, Joe would finally earn some money. Roxborough and Black brought him to Chicago and rented him a room in chef Bill Bottom's apartment.

From the start, Joe had great affection for his new trainer, Jack Blackburn. Joe nicknamed him Chappie—and followed his every command. Chappie got Joe out of bed at dawn to run six miles around Washington Park. When Joe finished, Chappie let him go back to bed and sleep until eleven, at which point Bottom would feed him a special hot breakfast of three broiled lamb chops, two soft-boiled eggs, two slices of toast, a large honeydew melon, and a cup of tea. The new regimen wrapped Joe in a solid layer of muscle. The young fighter soon grew out of his light heavyweight body and into a six-foot-two, 180-pound frame. He had become a true heavyweight.

At the gym, Chappie schooled Joe on the aspects of boxing that champions had down cold: positioning his feet, balancing his body weight, using momentum to triple his power. Chappie drilled Joe on shuffling backward and forward and on the most effective ways of blocking punches.

"There's no easy road to the top," he told Joe. "And for a colored fighter, it's even tougher. You've got to be good—lots better than the other man . . . You can't get nowhere nowadays trying to outpoint fellows in the ring. It's mighty hard for a colored boy to win decisions. The dice is loaded against you. You gotta knock 'em out and keep knocking 'em out to get anywheres. Let your right fist be the referee."

In other words, Joe wasn't going to get any favors from the judges. There were several ways to win a boxing match. Fights went fifteen rounds. To win on points, a boxer had to land more punches than his opponent, as tallied by the judges. To win by knockout, a fighter had to floor his opponent for ten seconds before the end of the final round. Chappie knew the judges weren't going to allow a black fighter to accumulate points. Joe would have to knock his opponents down for the count.

This kind of racism was no surprise to Joe. Boxers usually climbed the ranks by fighting as often as possible and beating tougher opponents along the way. Once a boxer proved himself worthy, he would get a title shot. But the highest echelons of professional boxing had been closed to blacks in the United States since the early 1900s.

There had been only one exception. In 1908, Canadian fighter Tommy Burns agreed to defend his world heavyweight title against the black challenger, Jack Johnson. No state in America would sanction the bout, so the two squared off in Sydney, Australia. As it turned out, Johnson outboxed the champion at every turn, battering him so badly that in the fourteenth round the police jumped in to stop the carnage.

To whites, Johnson was the devil. In an era when black men could be lynched just for looking at a white woman, Johnson married three of them. He openly taunted the establishment by flashing a gold tooth, dressing in fancy clothes, speeding in expensive cars, and gloating over his fallen opponents. There were even some in the African American community who were wary of Johnson's interracial romances, but to most blacks Johnson was a symbol of pride, brazen enough to stand up to white authority. To them, his defiance was a militant political protest against unequal treatment.

White promoters were so eager to see a white man beat Johnson that they tracked down former champion

Jim Jeffries on his alfalfa farm and lured him out of retirement.

The Johnson-Jeffries fight was held July 4, 1910, and it quickly became the most publicized sporting event to date. Once it started, it was clear to everyone watching that Jeffries was a better farmer than he was a boxer. Johnson pummeled Jeffries as badly as he had Tommy Burns, and after the third knockdown in the fifteenth round, the referee proclaimed Johnson the winner. As soon as news of Johnson's victory flashed over the wires, race riots broke out in cities across the country. White thugs—embarrassed and humiliated over the outcome—took out their anger on innocent black men. In Atlanta, Georgia, they attacked a black man who was cheering for Johnson. In Houston, Texas, they slashed the throat

Jack Johnson with Etta Duryea in 1910. They would marry in 1911.

of a black man on a streetcar. In New York City, they set fire to a tenement and tried to barricade the exits so the residents couldn't escape.

So, when Joe Louis stepped into the ring at Bacon's Casino in Chicago for his first professional fight—twenty-four years after Johnson had defeated Jeffries—he was aiming for a knockout. Fighting worn-out heavyweight Jack Kracken, Joe opened the fight by moving in on his opponent, forcing him to drop his guard, and pounding him on the jaw with a left hook. Kracken hit the canvas for a nine count, one second short of a knockout. He was barely back on his feet when Joe's right hand sent him sailing through the ropes and into the lap of the chairman of the Illinois State Athletic Commission. Before Joe had even broken a sweat, the fight was over—as was Kracken's career.

A week later, Joe nailed Willie Davies in the third round, opening a cut over Davies's eye, which prompted the referee to end the fight.

Two weeks after that, Joe popped Larry Udell on the chin in the second round. Udell dropped to the canvas. Like Kracken, he staggered to his feet just as the referee hit the count of nine. But in this case, Udell couldn't go on, and the fight was over.

Fighting on a brisk schedule of roughly two bouts per month, Joe knocked down opponents as quickly as his handlers lined them up. He was 11–0 within months of starting out, and newspapers in the Midwest were already talking about the young "Negro" fighter with fists of iron. One sports columnist predicted that if Joe could beat his next opponent, Lee Ramage, the former heavyweight champion of California, he'd be in "serious consideration as a contender for championship honors."

Joe didn't disappoint. In the eighth round, he battered Ramage to the canvas three times—the final blow coming by way of a crashing right to the chin. The media ate it up, praising Joe for displaying the "coolness of a frozen cucumber."

In seven months, Joe had skyrocketed from a hopeful amateur to a legitimate contender. He'd also gone from having empty pockets to a well-padded wallet. He knew right away what he'd do with the money—he went home with gifts and watches for his family.

"That was a swell Christmas," he said. "We had a turkey with all the trimmings, and plenty of ice cream."

By spring 1935, Joe's ring earnings had soared to $18,000, and he was able to do even more: He bought his mother a house. That Easter, he surprised her with a four-bedroom home on McDougall Avenue on Detroit's east side, and outfitted it with furniture, a piano, and a radio.

The press, riding the Joe Louis bandwagon, came up with nicknames for the rising star, all having to do with the color of his skin. At various points, he was pegged the Dark Destroyer, the Sepia Socker, and the Coffee-Colored KO King. The name that stuck—and the one that would follow Joe throughout his career—was the Brown Bomber.

Despite the catchy nickname, Joe's skin color remained a concern for his managers. Roxborough and Black knew their fighter was rising in the ranks, but the lesson of Jack Johnson still loomed large. Roxborough figured white promoters might give Joe a title shot if he was willing to appease them. He handed Joe a list of dos and don'ts that Joe was to follow if he ever hoped to become champ. Don't be photographed with a white woman. Don't go to nightclubs alone. Don't take any fixed or easy fights. Don't gloat over a fallen opponent. Do maintain a deadpan expression in front of the cameras. Do live and fight clean.

Joe got the point. Actually, it was hard to miss. If he wanted a shot at the title, he had to show white America that he was willing to play by its rules. In other words, he wouldn't be another Jack Johnson.

CHAPTER 2

"Save Me, Joe Louis"

With all the roadblocks in front of him, Joe knew just how hard it would be to get a shot at the heavyweight title. But if he could defeat his next opponent, Primo Carnera—a six-foot-six, 260-pound Goliath who had held the title a year earlier—the world just might see that he deserved one.

In early June 1935, John Roxborough and Julian Black set up Joe's training camp in Pompton Lakes, New Jersey. The camp was twenty-five miles from New York City, but it felt like a million miles away. It was deep in the countryside, surrounded by green hills, lakes, and farmhouses. And the compound even came with some history. The main building, a mansion dating back to 1694, once hosted George Washington. But none of that mattered to Joe. What he liked was that the camp had few distractions, other than a steady stream of journalists who came by hunting for stories and photographs.

When they did, Joe always kept in mind the code of conduct handed to him by Roxborough—that is, he aimed to carry himself with dignity.

At one point, a news photographer asked Joe to pose eating watermelon, a food associated with the denigrating stereotype of an uncultured black person.

"Not me," Joe said.

"Come on, Joe."

"Not me."

"Don't you like watermelon?"

"Not for eatin'," Joe said. "Or for posin'."

Joe stayed in Pompton Lakes three weeks, sparring with the biggest heavyweights his trainers could find—heavyweights built like Primo Carnera.

One such sparring partner, Seal Harris, stood six-four and weighed 245 pounds. A writer for the *Pittsburgh Courier*, Chester Washington, watched them spar. "The high spot of the day's activities occurred during the exhibition bouts in the outdoor ring, when one of the Brown Bomber's famous left-hand corkscrew punches exploded on Seal Harris' chin and the Seal went down like the *Lusitania*," he wrote. After absorbing Joe's hooks and crosses for three weeks, Seal left the camp, telling a newsman, "I'm glad I'm getting out of here alive."

On June 25, the day of the fight, Joe took the train to New York City, well aware that the match was getting a lot of attention, some of it focusing on the Italian-born

Carnera being a personal favorite of Benito Mussolini, Italy's fascist dictator. Newspapers were already reporting that the power-hungry Mussolini had beefed up his military and was ready to invade Ethiopia—an act of aggression that had the world on edge.

"How I felt coming into New York's big Pennsylvania Station!" Joe said. "That big glass ceiling where you can look up into the skies. It makes even a big guy feel awful small. The crowd sweeps by you. And nobody seems to notice you. As I looked up, I said to myself, 'Well, Joe, you always wanted to aim high. Now you can try to hitch your wagon to a star.'"

When Joe left the station, he was taken to Yankee Stadium. Most of the country's public arenas were segregated, but here, sixty thousand fans of all races were making their way through the same turnstiles. As Joe got out of the car, a group of black middle-aged men rushed to his side, pumping his hand. It was then that Joe saw firsthand how important he'd become to the African American community.

Black Americans were rooting for him, pulling for him to knock out the big Italian bully. To them, Joe was a representation of hope, a walking symbol of what happens when a black man is given an opportunity. Such examples were rare—so few black men or women were allowed to achieve that kind of status—and Joe had conquered every challenge put in front of him. He was, at just twenty-one years old, the most famous black man in the country. To follow Joe, all his fans had to do was open any black-owned newspaper. There was Joe dining at a restaurant, Joe relaxing at training camp, Joe listening to music, Joe reading the Bible.

And the stories grew around him. In one, a black prisoner was about to be executed in North Carolina. Legend has it that as the poison gas was filling up the man's lungs, he cried out, "Save me, Joe Louis. Save me, Joe Louis!" People loved Joe so much that they chose to believe the story, even though it was probably invented.

An editor at the *Sunday Worker* asked his sportswriter, Ted Benson, to write a column describing how the black community idolized Joe. Benson wrote, "A single column cannot begin to describe the feeling of the man of color who watches a brown-skinned boy like Joe Louis, from Alabama, the most backward State in the union, fight his way up from the coal mine and the cotton field through strength of his body and mind." Benson went on to say, "When the Negro boy died in the North Carolina jail with Joe Louis' name on his lips, he was expressing the deep need of the Negro people for liberation from the bitter oppression which rests upon them. . . . He saw in him a symbol of the struggle of the Negro people for emancipation."

Outside Yankee Stadium, Joe was besieged with

Joe looks dapper as he gets into a new Ford sedan in 1935.

well-wishers urging him to show Mussolini, and white America, what a black man could do.

Afraid of saying the wrong thing, Joe shook their hands but kept his mouth shut. He was equally tight-lipped when speaking to the press in his dressing room. He figured he'd let his fists do the talking. Still, when he climbed into the ring and saw Carnera, he couldn't help but wonder if he'd had too much faith in his own abilities. The Italian was four inches taller than Joe and looked even bigger in person.

"I almost needed a stepladder to get up to tag his chin," Joe said.

So when the bell rang, instead of attacking, Joe kept his eye on Carnera's fists, trying to avoid them, and worked to get inside and punch away at the big man's body. For five rounds, Joe's plan worked beautifully. He manhandled the oversized Carnera, knocking him to the ropes, battering his body with rapid combinations, then moving up to his head. At the end of the fifth round, Carnera wobbled to his corner, blood streaming down his massive chest. But at the start of the sixth, Carnera seemed to come back to life—only to be knocked down three times. After the third fall, he couldn't go on.

Upon hearing the news, black fans throughout the country celebrated another Joe Louis victory.

One of those fans was future poet, writer, and civil rights activist Maya Angelou. In her memoir, *I Know Why the Caged Bird Sings*, Angelou recounted listening to Joe's fights on the radio in Stamps, Arkansas. Neighbors would cram into her grandmother's grocery, the only black-owned store in town. Folks sat anywhere they could find a seat—on wooden crates, empty countertops, step stools. Mothers held babies on their laps; men leaned on shelves or one another. Maya's uncle Willie would turn up the volume so people on the porch wouldn't miss a punch.

Angelou explained the disappointment she'd feel whenever Joe got knocked down. She feared the sight of Joe on his knees would validate what racists ignorantly assumed to be true: that African Americans were biologically inferior to whites.

"My race groaned," she wrote about the prospect of Joe dropping to the canvas. "It was our people falling. It was another lynching, yet another Black man hanging on a tree. . . . If Joe lost, we were back in slavery and beyond help. It would all be true, the accusations that we were lower types of human beings. Only a little higher than the apes. . . . We didn't breathe. We didn't hope. We waited."

Angelou had no such concerns on the night of the Carnera fight. Joe had done it. He had beaten the Italian Goliath, defeated Mussolini, and given black Americans a hero of their own, somebody who just might be able to pull them out of their second-class citizenship.

But bigger tests were yet to come.

A Date with Max Baer

Joe was box-office gold. He'd won all twenty-one of his fights, and the public was clamoring for the twenty-second. The Brown Bomber filled stadiums wherever he fought—New York, Los Angeles, Chicago, Detroit—and was earning the kind of paydays usually reserved for Hollywood stars.

But no matter how spectacular he was in the ring, Joe remained remarkably unspectacular outside of it. Following manager John Roxborough's code of conduct, Joe never flashed his wealth, never shamed an opponent, never publicly socialized with white women, and never offended white America. Roxborough figured that if Joe stayed humble and kept winning, he just might land a title shot despite his skin color.

Joe was such a model citizen that he even attracted the attention of President Roosevelt. On August 27, 1935, the president met with Joe at the White House and handed him an autographed photo. He complimented Joe on his boxing skills, and congratulated him on his most recent victory, a first-round knockout of King Levinsky.

"He asked me a lot of questions about myself," Joe said. "[He] didn't seem in a hurry to let me go. He made me double-up my arm so he could feel my muscle and he said to me, 'Joe, you certainly are a fine-looking young man.'"

A few weeks later, Joe stood in the parlor of a friend's apartment in Harlem. It was September 24, and in three hours, he was due to fight Max Baer, the ex-champion who'd lost his title to James Braddock only months earlier. To Joe's left was his nineteen-year-old fiancée, Marva Trotter, the daughter of a minister. Marva had grown up in a middle-class family in Chicago; she'd hoped to become a dress designer, but after graduating from high school, studied stenography at one of the few schools that accepted African Americans. Today, she wore a simple, white wedding dress.

"I do," Joe said, in front of the small gathering.

This was their wedding, but the honeymoon would

have to wait. Joe had a pressing engagement with Max Baer's right hand, the same powerful brick that had pounded Primo Carnera to the canvas eleven times in as many rounds.

When the short ceremony ended, Joe headed out of the apartment with Roxborough. Before shutting the door, he told his wife and guests, "I've a date with a fellow named Max Baer."

Harlem was home to a quarter million blacks so it was only natural that hundreds of local residents would be gathered outside the building to cheer on the man who'd come to represent their race.

As he left the building, Joe waved to the crowd and then ducked into a waiting police cruiser. Within seconds, the cops whisked him off to the Bronx, and with the help of a blaring siren, delivered him to Yankee Stadium in time for the ten o'clock showdown.

When Baer climbed into the ring and took off his robe, nobody could miss the large white Star of David emblazoned on his dark trunks, not even the fans in the upper tier. The Nebraska-born ex-champ was only one-quarter Jewish and didn't observe the religion, but his manager, Ancil Hoffman, had suggested that Baer promote his heritage for marketing reasons. Baer started wearing the star in 1933, the same year Adolf Hitler and his Nazi regime came to power in Germany. By exploiting

Fans in Harlem hope to catch a glimpse of newlyweds Joe and Marva.

Baer's Judaism, Hoffman reasoned, the boxer could ride America's wave of anti-Nazi sentiment.

The New York papers had been full of stories about Hitler's persecution of Jews. After becoming German chancellor, Hitler had made it his mission to rid Germany of what he considered racial "undesirables." At first there were government-sponsored boycotts of Jewish-owned businesses, then he barred Jews from government service, limited Jewish students in public schools, and restricted the practice of Jewish doctors and lawyers. Now, in September 1935, after their conference in Nuremberg, the Nazis announced new anti-Jewish laws. They stripped the country's 500,000 Jews of German citizenship and made it illegal for them to marry someone of "German or related blood." American Jewish groups were calling for a national boycott of German goods and pressuring the U.S. government to officially condemn the actions of Hitler's Nazi regime.

Hoffman's strategy worked. Baer had countless Jewish fans, especially in New York City, which was home to nearly two million Jews. Even on the night he lost his title to Braddock, when nearly everybody in the arena was pulling for the Irishman, Baer had garnered the support of Jewish fans.

But when Joe made his way through the ropes at Yankee Stadium, it was clear he owned the crowd.

Max Baer wears the Star of David while fighting Joe.

A thunderous roar filled the air, and Joe raised his hand to acknowledge the packed house while sizing up his opponent. To Joe, Baer looked "as trim as a greyhound and as tanned as a hickory nut."

When the bell rang, Joe approached him warily, leading with his left. Baer, bent slightly at the waist, countered with his own left, keeping his powerful right cocked by his hip. Joe looked for an opening, a way to land a solid blow without running into that right fist. At the end of the third round, he found it, connecting squarely with two rights of his own. *Pow! Pow!* Baer crumpled to the canvas. When he got up, Joe caught him again, this time with three consecutive left hooks to the jaw. *Bam. Bam. Bam.* The ex-champ fell a second time, and referee Arthur Donovan started the count. One. Two. Three. When he reached four, the bell rang, ending the round and saving Baer from a near-certain knockout. Both fighters retreated to their corners, but the one-minute break wasn't enough to energize Baer.

In the fourth, Joe smashed him with a lunging right hand and a short, left hook, sending him to the canvas. Baer, his mind dazed, his body rubbery, managed to get up on one knee.

Jack Dempsey, who was working Baer's corner, implored him to stand up and fight, but Baer was too far gone to respond. He shook his head from side to side, trying to right himself, as Donovan stood over him, counting.

This time, there was no bell to save him. The count hit ten and the fight was over.

The crowd cheered wildly, whistling, clapping, calling Joe's name. The Brown Bomber was still undefeated.

To fully understand what Joe's success meant to the African American community, consider that five days after the Baer fight Joe went back to Detroit's Calvary Baptist Church—the same church he'd attended as a boy in Sunday school. There, 2,500 Brown-Bomber-loving churchgoers packed the inside of the place, and another 5,000 waited outside. When Joe showed up with his new bride, the throng, much like the one at Yankee Stadium, let out a roar—but the applause wasn't for Joe's conquests in the ring. The congregation was praising him for his clean living, and Joe responded by dropping a $100 bill into the collection box. More revealing, Rev. James S. Mastin called Joe a "good Christian boy" and said the young boxer had done more with his God-given talent than any other Negro since Lincoln freed the slaves.

Boxing insiders agreed. If Joe was white, he'd surely be on his way to a title fight. But the New York State Athletic Commission—the agency that governed boxing and made such decisions—still wasn't ready for a black champion. Instead, it threw another roadblock between Joe and the title.

The roadblock's name was Max Schmeling.

CHAPTER 3

Fourteen Years Earlier, Hamburg

In 1921, when Max Schmeling turned fifteen, he quit high school and got a job as a messenger at an advertising agency near his family's apartment in Hamburg, Germany. Max's job was easy—all he had to do was deliver materials to the local newspapers, the *Hamburgischer Korrespondent* and the *Hamburger Nachrichten*—but it was boring. The only part of the job he liked was polishing his boss's Isotta Fraschini, an Italian luxury car that had a powerful engine, four shiny spoked wheels, and big, fat chrome headlamps. Max's father had been a sailor and spent the Great War guarding the coast of Germany. Now he earned a meager salary as a navigator for the Hamburg-American steamship line. Like most everyone in Germany, which was mired in an economic depression, the family needed every cent it could scrounge together. Max was even pitching in his money from the agency. Any kind of luxury, let alone an Isotta Fraschini, was obviously out of the question.

As he rubbed the rag over that gleaming grille, all he could think about was getting in a boxing ring. His father had told him about the many fights he'd seen in his travels, and Max, hearing about the fame and money, was more than intrigued. And so, after work, he raced to the local movie theater, which he'd done every night for a week, to watch Jack Dempsey defend his heavy-weight title against French boxer Georges Carpentier. He sat under the projectionist's window and leaned forward to catch every second of the fourth round. He knew it by heart: Dempsey, that bobbing, weaving, American locomotive, throwing that blurry left hook and following it with that short, lightning-quick right; Carpentier dropping to the canvas and then jumping to his feet at the count of nine; Dempsey landing a left to the face and Carpentier stumbling; Dempsey driving a sledge-hammer into Carpentier's ribs and then another to the jaw; Carpentier tumbling to the canvas; the ref standing over him and counting; Carpentier unable to get up. Then—with the fight over at one minute and sixteen seconds into the round—Dempsey walking over to the fallen Frenchman and helping him to his corner. What a champion.

In that theater Max promised himself that he would get into a boxing ring, if only to feel the canvas under his feet. Max had wrestled, swum, and played soccer in school. Strong and husky, he started doing push-ups, sit-ups, and calisthenics to build up his muscles. He bought himself a pair of used boxing gloves. The leather was worn and patched, but Max loved them.

One day, when Max was carrying advertising proofs to the *Hamburgischer Korrespondent*, the elevator man inside the building told him he had to take the stairs. Max refused. Why should he have to lug those bulky proofs? The man pushed him, so Max reared back and socked the operator, sending him to the floor—just like Dempsey had done to Carpentier.

It was his first knockout. It was also his first firing, because the incident cost him his job. It didn't matter, though, because Max's mind had turned away from advertising.

He was going to become a boxer.

Chasing Dempsey

When it came to idolizing Dempsey, Max wasn't alone—fight fans everywhere looked up to the champ. Dempsey's feats were legendary. He'd been a real-life hobo jumping onto moving freight trains and riding underneath the cars. He'd flattened one opponent in twenty-three seconds. He'd knocked out another with one punch. He'd taken the heavyweight title from a fighter fifty-six pounds heavier. He even had a great nickname, the Manassa Mauler. By

1923, Dempsey was drawing hundreds of thousands of fans to his fights. When he beat Luis Firpo to keep his title, he knocked the Argentinean down seven times in one round. For that fight he made nearly half a million dollars. Even the great Babe Ruth, the highest-paid player in baseball, only made $52,000 a year playing for the New York Yankees.

Max knew if he was going to amount to anything in the boxing ring, he had to leave Hamburg to do it. So, he gathered his small savings and headed for the city of Cologne. Along the way, he tramped through the countryside, finding work in various towns. To save money, he ate in soup kitchens and slept in lodging houses—not on a bed, but on a long wooden board anchored to a brick wall. Eventually, he went to work as a strongman in the circus performing superhuman feats: He bent spikes with his bare hands, drove nails through boards with his fists, and lifted iron weights with his teeth. He even did a stunt where he lay down and let cars drive over him. His muscles were as hard as stone.

The circus closed after nine months, though, leaving Max stranded in Cologne. He landed a job with bricklayers in the nearby suburb of Mühleim, and one night they took him to see the fights at a local boxing club. Max returned again and again. Eventually, a club official noticed the muscular young man and suggested Max get in the ring himself. The instant he stepped through the ropes,

Max's regular calisthenics strengthened his body for boxing.

Max knew he'd found what he'd been looking for: a boxing home. He began fighting at the club in the evenings, and working out whenever he got the chance, teaching himself the basics: footwork, punching, bobbing, weaving. And he lived clean—no smoking, drinking, partying, or girls.

In 1924, when Max was eighteen, he was skilled enough to reach the finals of Germany's amateur boxing championships. Fighting as a light heavyweight, he lost the match, but soon went pro, convinced that his overhand right would be a powerful weapon if he kept working on it.

A year later, he met his hero in person when Dempsey showed up in Cologne to put on a boxing exhibition. As Dempsey's train pulled into the station, Max was there to greet it. He muscled his way through the crowd and

Jack Dempsey and second wife, actress Estelle Taylor, pillars of sports and Hollywood celebrity.

introduced himself to the champ. It was his dream, he said, to box with Dempsey. Then he asked if he could go one round with the champ during the exhibition. Impressed with Max's enthusiasm, Dempsey agreed.

When Max entered the ring, in front of a throng of cheering Dempsey fans, he pictured himself fighting for the world title. But once the exhibition began, it was all he could do to survive. Dempsey owned the ring as a ballerina does a dance floor, entertaining the crowd and whacking Max with short, stunning blows. The bell couldn't ring soon enough for Max. When it did, he returned to his corner, his face drenched in sweat. As he sat there, sucking in huge gulps of air, Dempsey walked over and congratulated him on his courage. If Max trained hard, Dempsey said, he'd be a great boxer one day.

That's all Max needed to hear. With Dempsey's words swirling around in his head, he decided he was ready for tougher competition. So for the second time in his life, he packed up all his possessions, stuffed his gym clothes and boxing gloves into a cardboard box, and bought a train ticket—this time, to Berlin.

Max's Rise

The big city was a hotbed of activity, chock-full of cabarets, dance halls, beer gardens, museums, and movie houses. Artists, writers, and musicians gravitated to Berlin, and people of all shapes and sizes, including 160,000 Jews, called it home.

There, Max focused on his craft. He set out to pack even more power into his right hand, to make it as potent as Dempsey's. He hooked up with a trainer, Max Machon, who put him on a grueling regimen. Soon, the young fighter was waking up at six in the morning, running ten miles through the woods, sprinting up hills in hundred-meter bursts, and lifting weights. It wasn't long before Max became a different fighter, bigger and stronger than ever before.

From March 1926 to May 1927, Max won twelve straight bouts, ten by knockout. Then in June, he defeated Belgian Fernand Delarge to win the European light heavyweight title. It was official: Max Schmeling, at twenty-one years old, was the best light heavyweight in Europe. When he raised his gloves in victory, the German fans rose to their feet, chanting his name over and over, bursting with pride as they saluted their countryman.

As Max piled up victories, he gained an even bigger following. Germans of all classes turned out in huge numbers to see the country's young sensation. When Max beat Italian champion Michele Bonaglia at the Sports Palace in Berlin, fans treated him as if he was a war hero, clapping, cheering, and singing Germany's national anthem, "Deutschlandlied."

Max was quickly becoming the toast of Berlin society, and he loved the adulation. He posed for artists and sculptors who saw his muscular physique as the epitome of the human male form. He attended art galleries, theatrical openings, and fancy parties, dressed in high-priced suits from David Lewin's fashionable Prince of Wales clothing shop. And he was a regular at the Roxy Sportsbar, a popular hangout for athletes and celebrity sports fans.

By 1928, Max was supporting himself but itching for bigger paydays—and bigger headlines. He beefed up in weight, gaining nearly ten pounds, and set out for the German heavyweight title. When promoters announced that Max would take on the champ, Franz Diener, on April 4, the match became so highly anticipated that one Berlin theater rescheduled the opening of a play for the following night.

On the evening of the match, the arena was a mob

Schmeling, dressed to the max.

scene. Max made his way to the back entrance, winding around the crowds on Potsdamer Strasse, and saw tickets being scalped at six times their face value.

Max weighed in at 181, but was the lighter man by twelve pounds. He came out swinging and didn't let up, not even after fracturing his left thumb in the first minutes of the bout. It was fifteen rounds of action, and in the end, Max took the title, having outscored Diener on points. The crowd drowned him in cheers, and Max happily soaked up the adulation, ignoring the throbbing pain in his left hand.

Max now owned the European light heavyweight and German heavyweight crowns. Since the European heavyweight champion was inactive, the only high-stakes title left was the world heavyweight championship. For that, he'd have to compete on boxing's biggest stage: the United States of America.

New York City, 1928

Max stood at the railing of the 600-foot-long ocean liner *New York* as it steamed into the harbor. The city was so much bigger than in picture books and on postcards. The Statue of Liberty towered over the water, and skyscrapers reached into the clouds over lower Manhattan. Men and women waited on the pier, waving excitedly to the ship's passengers. When the boat docked, dozens of reporters and photographers rushed aboard, their bags and cameras slung over their shoulders as they tried to spot famous people to put in the next morning's edition.

The clamorous scene made Max even more enthusiastic about having left Germany. It was way too soon to think about fighting for the title—it takes time to climb the rankings—but if Max was ever going to do it, this would be the place.

"Before me rose America, the world's boxing crown, and riches exceeding my early dreams," Max said, adding that he was "light of heart and eager to test my strength against the fighting men on the other side of the Atlantic."

Once settled, Max went to see a surgeon to get his thumb repaired. Dr. Wilfred Fralick, a specialist who'd operated on many high-profile boxers, found a small piece of bone floating near the thumb's joint. Fralick removed it, and gave Max the green light to begin training once his finger healed.

The doctor was so impressed by Max's physique that he told one sportswriter, "The boy has a splendid pair of fighting hands, or will have when he recovers from this operation, and a jaw capable of withstanding the kick of a mule."

After spending a few months recuperating, Max was ready to get back in the ring. But in New York boxing circles, he was a nobody, and it was tough to find a manager with the right kind of connections. So he pushed aside his German manager in favor of Joe Jacobs, a fedora-wearing, cigar-chomping, fast-talking boxing insider known by his Yiddish name, Yussel. Jacobs, the son of Hungarian Jews born in New York City's Lower East Side, was so well connected—and had so much pull in the fight game—that nearly everyone referred to him as Yussel the Muscle. For Max, Jacobs was the ideal manager. Besides being familiar with the inner workings of the sport, especially in New York, he was an out-and-out publicity hound. Max figured that Jacobs wouldn't let him disappear in the flood of wannabes coming out of the local gyms.

He was right.

First, Jacobs gave his client a nickname, the Black Uhlan of the Rhine. Black referred to his hair; uhlans were the cavalry riders of the historical kingdom of Prussia in northern Germany. The name wasn't exactly apt since Max had grown up nowhere near the Rhine River, but the fighter didn't seem to care—as long as it helped get his name in the papers.

Next, Jacobs introduced Max to the public. He shoved him in front of as many cameras as possible. He had the Black Uhlan visit kids at local schools and shake hands with politicians. He even had him pose for photographers on top of skyscrapers. And he always played up how his fighter mimicked Dempsey's style in the ring— crouching, bobbing, weaving, stalking his opponent like a feral cat, pouncing with both fists. What better way to get the public to think of his boy as a champion?

The campaign worked like a charm. The name Max Schmeling started getting around, and soon promoters at the all-important Madison Square Garden agreed to arrange a match with Boston fighter Joe Monte. It went just as Jacobs had hoped: Max knocked out Monte in the eighth round.

"What a right hand!" Tex Rickard, the promoter of the fight, shouted afterward.

True enough, Max's right had been his biggest weapon. But it had also been his only weapon. The next day, a sportswriter referred to Max's left hand as merely something for holding a fork.

Former world heavyweight champion James J. Corbett agreed. After watching the Schmeling-Monte fight, Corbett said that Max looked crude and needed to develop his left. And he made it clear that Max was no Jack Dempsey. No fighter could rise to the top of the ranks without a "superb left-handed attack," Corbett said.

But Max continued to inch up the rankings. Two months after beating Monte, he outpointed Ohio heavyweight Joe Sekyra in ten rounds. Less than three weeks later, he dispensed with Pietro Corri in the first round.

Jacobs felt that his fighter was ready for the big time, and he set up a match between Max and the tough-as-nails Johnny Risko. The twenty-six-year-old Risko, who worked in his family's bakery, would surely be Max's toughest challenge since coming to America.

The match was held at Madison Square Garden on February 1, 1929, and Max was in trouble from the start. When the bell rang, he rushed at Risko, only to be greeted by a thunderous blow to his jaw. Things didn't get easier from there. The next few rounds, Max would later say, were the hardest of his career.

But after that, Risko showed signs of tiring, and Max seized on the opportunity to make his move. He went at Risko with his right hand, hammering him over and over, flooring him in the seventh, again in the eighth, and again in the ninth. Finally, referee Arthur Donovan stopped the fight. The crowd cheered for Max so mightily—and so wildly—that it took a squad of police officers to clear a safe path to his dressing room.

"Donovan raised my hand and in all my life I do not

believe I heard such cheering," Max said. "I was a hero! The great crowd applauded me as though I were one of their own. It was a wonderful feeling."

The Black Uhlan was now on the map, besieged with interview requests from magazines, newspapers, and radio reporters. His picture popped up on sports pages around the country. Fans stopped him on the street, hoping for a handshake or an autograph.

Four months later, on June 27, 1929, Max beat the Spanish-born Paulino Uzcudun—finally putting himself in line for the title. The only problem was there was no champion to fight. The titleholder, Gene Tunney, had retired after beating Dempsey. And so the New York State Athletic Commission arranged for Max to face the number one contender, Jack Sharkey. The winner would become the world heavyweight champion.

CHAPTER 4

Foul!

June 12, 1930. Streams of excited boxing fans made their way through the turnstiles at Yankee Stadium. Celebrities, including former champions Dempsey and Tunney, filled the high-priced seats around the ring. They had come to see Max battle Jack Sharkey for the title. The two fighters strutted into the ring. Max was decked out in Germany's national colors: black, red, and gold. Sharkey was draped in the American flag.

This was Max's shot, the moment he'd been waiting for. No German had ever won the world heavyweight championship. But as soon as the bell rang, it was clear Sharkey, a seasoned ring veteran three years older than Max, wanted the title just as badly. Sharkey came out throwing sharp punches, stinging Max with laserlike lefts and rights, and after the first few rounds was well ahead on points. Toward the end of the fourth, Sharkey backed into the ropes. Max rushed in, but before he could land a solid right, Sharkey threw a left that landed well below Max's belt. It was a blatant rule-breaker, and when Max tumbled onto the canvas clutching his groin, Joe Jacobs saw a path to the title.

"Stay down! Foul!" the manager yelled as he crawled through the ropes and scrambled to his fighter. "You wuz fouled!"

Pandemonium erupted in the stands as spectators jumped out of their seats, screaming, hissing, and booing.

Sharkey's handlers raced into the ring and tugged on referee Jimmy Crowley's sleeve, demanding that he count out Schmeling.

Jacobs ran over and grabbed his other sleeve. "You won't count nobody out!" he shouted.

Crowley wriggled loose and went to confer with the judges. Moments later, the verdict was in: Max had won the fight by disqualification.

As James P. Dawson of the *New York Times* reported, "Sharkey was a pitiful figure in defeat. He was utterly crushed . . . shocked to speechlessness and incapable of action. His handlers raved and ranted, and all Sharkey did was stand motionless in his corner permitting his handlers to drape him with his navy blue bathrobe with the navy insignia on its back. Then he walked dejectedly from the ring, a crushed, disappointed figure if there ever was one."

Max wasn't much happier. In his heart he didn't feel

like a champion. Jacobs had won the fight for him on a technicality and was no doubt a genius for having done so. But Max wanted to take the title decisively; winning on a disqualification didn't feel like winning at all.

It turned out that German boxing fans agreed.

As Max remembered it, when he returned to Germany, the folks at home badgered him, constantly asking why he took the championship under such questionable circumstances. "If I had refused the title, people would have talked about me for three days," he said in response. "And on the fourth day, I would have been forgotten. But now the interest in the next fight [would] be great and it [would] bring in even more money than the first."

Joe Jacobs, ever-present cigar between his lips, admires Max's title belt.

But it didn't matter what the cynics, or anybody else, thought. In 1930, Max Schmeling was the first German in history to hold the world heavyweight title.

"We Was Robbed!"

After winning the title, when Max returned to Germany, he found a country slipping into economic despair. The Great Depression that began in America in 1929 had spread across the Atlantic. Like Americans, Germans were standing in bread lines and outside soup kitchens, starving, hoping to fill their stomachs with a bowl of broth or a hunk of day-old bread.

Frightened Germans were looking for answers, and Hitler promised his Nazi Party would bring order to the chaos and make Germany great again. He blamed Jews for the Depression and launched a relentless propaganda campaign highlighting the government's failures. In the 1930 elections, the Nazis secured a significant portion of the legislature—and by 1932 Hitler was making deals to gain more power.

At this point, Max was back in the United States. He'd successfully defended his title once, and was preparing for a rematch with Sharkey. He was determined to beat him fair and square.

The fight took place on June 21, 1932, at the Garden Bowl in New York City, and Max was in top shape. He battled Sharkey for fifteen rounds, throwing sharp punches and staying strong through the finish. So when the final bell rang, he figured he had won on points and fully expected to hear, "The winner and *still* champion, Max Schmeling!" But ring announcer Joe Humphreys seemed surprised when he saw the voting slips from the referee and the judges. Something wasn't right.

"The winner," Humphreys shouted, "and *new* champion, Jack Sharkey!"

The packed house at the outdoor arena erupted in boos and cheers as Sharkey reclaimed the belt many felt he never should have lost in the first place. Max was crestfallen, but he walked across the ring to congratulate the stunned, ecstatic champion.

Joe Jacobs stormed into the ring and grabbed a radio microphone.

"Ladies and gentlemen," he yelled. "We was robbed! We was robbed!"

Max figured that Jacobs must be wrong, that his manager was blinded by loyalty, that the judges had seen something Jacobs had missed. But the next day, when he picked up the local newspapers, Max read that in a poll of twenty-five American writers covering the fight, twenty-three thought he should have won.

He really had been robbed.

W. O. McGeehan of the *New York Herald Tribune* wrote, "It has been the legend that a foreign fighter could not get a square deal in the United States, especially in

New York. Up to this time I felt that this was merely a legend but the decision given last night proved different."

James P. Dawson of the *New York Times* agreed. "Schmeling won," he wrote, "because of a tireless, persistent, unswerving offensive launched at the opening bell and never once interrupted, even in the face of Sharkey's best blows."

Even Jimmy Walker, the mayor of New York, was enraged. He told a German reporter, "That is the rottenest decision I ever heard in my life." Walker then gave the reporter permission to translate his words for boxing fans in Germany.

Max sailed home again in October. He would not return to the United States for six months.

During that time, both countries were slogging through the Great Depression. President Roosevelt's efforts to pull America out of its economic tailspin included a massive public jobs program called the Work Projects Administration (WPA) that put people to work building roads, post offices, bridges, schools, and highways. Hitler, too, started a public works program, but at the same time was rearming the military as part of his ultimate plan to rule Europe in the name of the Germanic race, which he called the master Aryan race.

As soon as Hitler took power, the Nazis started rounding up political opponents, dissenters, and perceived threats to the regime—Communists, Freemasons, Jehovah's Witnesses—and banished them to concentration camps. The first was in Dachau, in southern Germany, but there would be thousands more as the Nazis would ultimately target racial "undesirables"—Jews, Roma, homosexuals, persons with physical or mental disabilities. The prisoners were beaten, starved, brutalized, and forced into slave labor. They were ordered to dig coal and stone from mines and quarries, and to build the walls and infrastructure of the camps themselves. In the coming war, the Nazis would add killing centers, and millions of prisoners would be systematically exterminated.

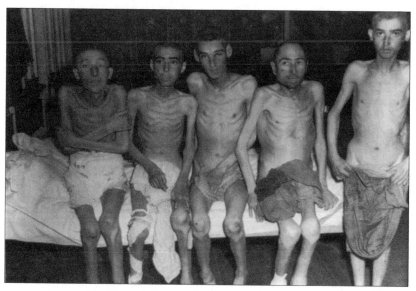

The first concentration camps opened in 1933. Few of the millions of prisoners sent there would survive.

In August 1934, Max visited his hometown of Hamburg. One night he joined his trainer Max Machon and some friends for dinner, and the conversation turned to the political situation in Germany. They talked about Hitler's ruthlessness and how it was affecting boxing. The führer, as Hitler called himself, had banished Jews from the sport and forced Jewish titleholders to give up their championship belts. Max wondered if his Jewish manager, Joe Jacobs, would ever dare visit Germany again.

"There was a moment in which it suddenly became clear to all of us what was happening," Max said years later. "The circle of friends, artists and actors, had long since scattered to the four winds; now reality was taking hold of sports as well, shattering bonds that had never cared about borders, skin color, or race."

Max had seen it happen firsthand. He'd married the famous Czechoslovakian actress Anny Ondra a year earlier, and watched as his wife had to shut down her production company when her Jewish business partners fled the country.

Max was torn between his loyalty to his friends and his allegiance to the Nazi regime. He never officially joined the Nazi Party, but his behavior during this time does suggest that he was complicit with it. He stayed in Germany and continued to rub shoulders with high-ranking Nazi officials. It's not clear why he made this choice—it's possible that he believed in Nazi ideals, or that he realized those

Max and Czech film star Anny Ondra on their wedding day, July 6, 1933.

relationships would help his social standing, and possibly save his career.

Because Max had a problem. At only twenty-nine, not much was going right for him in the ring. First, he had won the championship by default. Then he lost the rematch on a decision. He'd won his next fight, against Mickey Walker, but then he'd been knocked out by Max Baer in Yankee Stadium and outpointed by Steve Hamas in Philadelphia. His twelve-rounder against veteran Paulino Uzcudun in Spain had wound up in a draw.

Max asked Joe Jacobs to come to Germany to give him moral support for a rematch with Steve Hamas. Max was pretty sure that Jacobs would be safe from Hitler's tyranny if he wasn't there in an official capacity. But he was wrong. As Max remembered years later, when Jacobs arrived at Berlin's Hotel Bristol, the desk clerk refused him a room.

Max, standing beside Jacobs, flew into a rage.

"When this shows up in the New York papers," he yelled, "you'll have seen your last American guest. And you can be sure that my guests will never stay here again."

The clerk reluctantly caved, but the issue of Jacobs's race was far from dead.

A few nights later, after Max knocked out Hamas in the ninth round, the twenty-five thousand fans in Hamburg's Hanseatic Hall spontaneously stood, raised their arms in a Nazi salute, and burst into a chorus of Germany's national anthem. Jacobs ran into the ring to congratulate Max and instinctively joined the crowd, half-heartedly thrusting his right arm in the air, his ever-present cigar firmly planted between his thumb and forefinger.

"After a few seconds," Max said, "he turned to me and winked."

The incident was a mere moment in time, one that surely would have been forgotten if ringside photographers had not caught it on film. Within days, newspapers around the world were running images of the short Jewish man extending his arm in a Nazi salute. German officials saw the cigar as a sign of disrespect and accused Jacobs of mocking them.

After Max's defeat of Steve Hamas in Hamburg, Jewish manager Joe Jacobs (far right), cigar in hand, joins the Germans in a Nazi salute. The Nazi regime was not pleased.

In his own defense, Jacobs said he had simply gotten caught up in the moment. "What the hell would *you* do?" he said to a writer from the *New Yorker* magazine.

It wasn't long before Max was sitting across from the Reich's minister of sports, having been summoned by the minister himself, Hans von Tschammer. When Max arrived at Tschammer's office, he immediately caught sight of a pile of newspapers sitting on the desk, each displaying Jacobs's infamous salute.

The minister opened the meeting by telling Max that he should box more often in Germany, that he could be a wonderful role model for the country's young men. As he spoke, he picked up a wooden ruler and slapped it against his palm.

"It's dumb to burn all your bridges behind you!" he said.

Then, after a few more empty suggestions, Tschammer stood bolt upright, thrust his arm in the air, and proclaimed, "Heil Hitler."

The meeting was over, and Max left with the clear understanding that if he expected to fight in Germany, he'd have to fire his Jewish manager. In other words, behave or pay the price.

Max had no intention of submitting to the threat, but a few days later a letter landed in his mailbox. What Tschammer had not said in the meeting was now an official directive. You're the only German athlete who works with a Jew, Tschammer wrote. Rectify that situation. Now.

Max knew that Jacobs was his only hope to land big-money fights in the United States, so once again he turned to his friends in the Nazi Party. He requested an audience with Hitler and quickly received an invitation to tea. Bring your wife, the führer said.

Soon, Max and Anny were sitting at the Reich Chancellery, making small talk with Hitler over coffee and pastries. Max explained that he couldn't succeed in New York without Jacobs. Most important, Max said,

Jacobs is competent and respectable. When Hitler remained silent, Max added, "Besides, loyalty is a German virtue."

Hitler still didn't respond. Instead, the führer spent the rest of the meeting fawning over Anny. In his view, she was the perfect Aryan: blond and blue-eyed. It was an awkward visit, to say the least, ending when one of Hitler's guards ushered Max and Anny out of the room.

Max never heard any more objections about his Jewish manager, so he figured the issue was finally put to rest. And it was. But he soon found out that dealing with the führer was a two-way street. Just as he was about to return to America in the hopes of reclaiming his title, he received a call from Dr. Theodor Lewald of the German Olympic Committee. Hitler wanted a favor.

The country was gearing up for the 1936 Olympics in Berlin, which Hitler saw as a way to prove Aryan superiority. But there was a problem. Word of Hitler's actions—specifically, his arrest of Communists and harassment of Jews—was getting out. America and other countries were threatening a boycott. Lewald explained that the führer wanted Max to meet with Avery Brundage, the president of the U.S. Olympic Committee, and assure him that all participating athletes would be treated fairly in Germany. Max followed orders. Upon his return to New York, he met with Brundage and delivered the message: There will be no discrimination at the upcoming games.

Hitler's plan worked. Shortly after the meeting, the U.S. Olympic Committee took a vote and narrowly agreed to participate.

Satisfied that he had lived up to his end of the bargain with Hitler, Max turned his attention back to his career. In early December 1935, he headed over to the office of the New York State Athletic Commission and met with its members, as well as its chairman, Brigadier General John J. Phelan. Max had his heart set on fighting for the world championship, which was now held by James Braddock.

"Gentlemen," Max said in his best English, "will you permit me to fight Braddock for the title?"

Phelan wasn't about to hand Max, or any German, a shot at the belt.

"We regard you as an outstanding contender, of course," Phelan said. "But we feel you should first meet Joe Louis, who also merits such ranking. Therefore, our answer is no."

Max had been hearing a lot about Joe Louis, and frankly, he was tired of it. Yes, Louis was good, but what had he done that Max hadn't? A fighter with Max's credentials shouldn't have to fight a newbie like Louis. But Max was as much a pragmatist and businessman as he was a boxer. If he defeated Louis, he'd almost certainly get a shot at Braddock.

"All right," he said. "I will fight Louis."

"I Saw Something"

On December 13, 1935, Max sat ringside at Madison Square Garden, surrounded by a sellout crowd, watching the Brown Bomber go toe-to-toe with Paulino Uzcudun. Louis looked good, especially in the fourth round when he tagged Uzcudun's chin with a swift, powerful right uppercut.

Joe Williams of the *Pittsburgh Press* described the action: "A swift, hissing right hand almost literally tore the left side of Paulino's face off. . . . It could not have been any more destructive if it had been a hand grenade."

Uzcudun went down on his back and reached for the ropes. He pulled himself up and onto his feet, but his tank was empty. Louis landed two more blows, a left to the body and a right to the head, before referee Arthur Donovan stopped the fight.

It was the first time Max had seen Louis in action, and he was impressed. Still, he felt certain he would beat the kid next June. He would be faster than the thirty-six-year-old Uzcudun. And he'd hit harder.

While Uzcudun was led to his corner, his face bruised and swollen, his lips smeared with blood, a throng of reporters ran to Max, eager to get his take on the unbeatable Louis.

"So, what do you have to say now?" one reporter asked.

"Joe Louis is the hardest puncher that I've ever seen," Max said in his German-accented English. "Anyone who plans on beating him had better know what they're doing."

"No one stands between him and the championship, not you either, Max," said another reporter.

"Joe Louis still has a lot to learn," Max said.

The reporters chuckled. Why wouldn't they? Uzcudun, the same fighter who'd given Max trouble, was now being carried from the ring, his career finished. Plus, Louis was unbeaten, and Max had won only four out of his last eight fights.

"I saw something," Max blurted out.

The reporters chuckled in disbelief. "What was it?" one of them asked. "What did you see, Max?"

Max didn't answer. Instead, he told the reporters they'd have to wait to find out. "I'll show you how to beat Joe Louis," he said.

When Max woke up the next morning, his words were splashed across every sports page he could find. America couldn't wait to see what Max had up his sleeve, and whether he could actually drop the great Brown Bomber.

A day later, Schmeling and his trainer Max Machon

left for Germany to come up with a game plan. Max was carrying two suitcases.

One contained his clothes.

The other was weighed down with films of Joe Louis fights.

CHAPTER 5

Joe's Training Camp

The Schmeling fight promised to be the easiest $300,000 Joe ever earned. Since turning pro two years earlier, he had beaten everybody put in front of him—and he had added another eighteen pounds of pure muscle along the way. The weight hadn't slowed him down. If anything, it had packed even more power into his fists, if such a thing was possible. Heading into his showdown against Schmeling, Joe had scored seven straight knockouts, two of them against ex-champs, Primo Carnera and Max Baer.

Schmeling, on the other hand, hadn't fought in nearly a year. And at the age of thirty, he was, in boxing terms, about a month younger than a Tyrannosaurus rex.

Still, Joe saw no reason to be boastful.

Joe Williams of the *Pittsburgh Press* wrote that the only vanity he spotted in the young fighter came in the form of tailored clothes. It was true; Joe was going through a lot of his cash, much of it on clothing. He'd just bought ten new suits, bringing his total to thirty for the year. For Joe, an expensive wardrobe was a reminder that he was no longer penniless and that his days of wearing hand-me-downs were over.

"I spent a lot on fancy clothes when I got big money," Joe said years later. "That was because I was so raggedy when I was a kid. One time I had around 100 suits made by Billy Taub in New York and MacIntosh in Hollywood. They stood me $150 to $185 apiece, made to order."

Joe's ambitions didn't end there.

"Well, I got my mother all fixed up nice, with a home, an automobile and a bank account," he said. "For myself, I want to get me a nice big farm in the country where I can raise chickens and cows and things, and have a lot of horses to ride. And I'd like to run a drugstore somewhere. I like drugstores."

In preparation for the Schmeling fight, Joe moved his training camp to the resort town of Lakewood, New Jersey, fifty miles south of New York City. When he arrived—looking sharp in a wide-lapelled suit and broad-brimmed fedora—fans ran to him eager for an autograph. Joe happily obliged, signing his name on cards, newspapers, whatever was thrust at him. By now, he had also become more relaxed around the press. He chatted with the usual contingent of reporters, patiently answering questions about his health, his sleep schedule, his diet, his celebrity visitors, his right cross, and his wife Marva's comings and goings.

Everything Joe did and said was reported—except his extramarital shenanigans. Those were kept secret from the public, and from Marva.

"I don't know where they get this idea that women are the weaker sex, and that they're shy," he said years later. "My God, the women, the starlets, White and Black, came jumping at me. I was the weaker sex. I didn't resist one pretty girl who had a sparkle in her eye."

Updates from Joe's training camp were broadcast via radio wire to New York on Monday, Wednesday, Saturday, and Sunday nights. (Reports from Schmeling's camp went out on Tuesday, Thursday, and Friday nights.) Most writers agreed that Joe was in the best shape of his life. He'd been out of the ring for a few months—taking it easy and working on his golf game—but at twenty-two, his speed, his power, and his reflexes were as good as ever. The fight was going to be a cakewalk.

At camp, Joe put on his trunks and climbed into the ring for regular sparring sessions, often held outdoors before thousands of onlookers. The idea was to put Joe in the ring with boxers who would replicate Schmeling's style in one way or another. They were paid $25 a day for their labors. One round was with a Chicagoan named Roy Williams. His job was to move as quickly as the German, and when the bell rang, he weaved to his right and left, creating a swiftly moving target. Joe swung and missed—twice—but he soon zeroed in on the bull's-eye. He unleashed lethal combinations on the 175-pound Williams, who quickly found a home on the ropes, cowering behind his gloves.

Another victim was ring veteran Salvatore Ruggirello. Unlike Williams, Ruggirello came straight at Joe. He threw heavy punches, but Joe responded with hard, stiff jabs and three- and four-punch combinations. After a few minutes, Ruggirello, now little more than a human shock absorber, staggered out of the ring, a pulpy mess. When an assistant trainer pleaded with him to come back for another turn, Ruggirello was so battered that the only word he could get out was no.

Mushky Jackson, who ran the training camp, tried in vain to get Joe to lighten up on his sparring mates.

"I bring 'em in here, but they don't last but a day," Jackson said. "That Louis busts their brains out. He's worse'n Dempsey ever was. When he knocks 'em down he picks 'em up and says, 'You feeling all right?' If they so much as nod their wobbling heads he lets 'em loose and whacks again. . . . They get out as soon as they can."

One sparring partner, Frank Schildknecht, had fought Joe in the amateurs. "You can see that left coming, but you can't do nothing about it," he told a reporter after eating his share of leather. "He almost killed me in

Joe sets off on his roadwork with trainer Chappie Blackburn (center) and assistant trainer Larry Amadee.

the amateurs, but [now] he's more polished. . . . I'm glad I ain't Schmeling."

Word of Joe's punishments made their way to Schmeling, who was training in the cool, remote air of Napanoch, a small town at the foothills of the Catskills in upstate New York. Speculation was that Joe Jacobs had set up his fighter's camp at the local Jewish country club in order to avoid the stigma of Nazism that was starting to cling to Schmeling.

Schmeling showed little concern over Joe knocking down sparring partners like bowling pins.

"Nobody has ever hit Joe Louis a real hard punch," Schmeling said. "Maybe that's why they call him a super-fighter. But I will hit him. Let me tell you."

Schmeling was confident. "I did not come across the water to lose," he often said.

Joe was an 8-1 favorite, and the odds were still climbing. As fight night approached, the only question on the minds of most experts was how long Schmeling would last.

Sports columnist Jimmy Cannon thought differently; he worried that money may have softened Joe's desire. "Hunger is the fighter's friend," he wrote. "Success and plenty are his enemies. Instead of the relentless kid fighting for his life, Joe is now a guy fighting for money in the bank, another car, another suit, another day in the sun over Lakewood."

It was true that Joe had cut some sparring sessions short and sneaked off to the golf course more often than he should have, but most everyone—admirers, writers, handlers—agreed he was invincible.

When the fight was postponed a day because of rain, the experts asked, Will the odds go even higher? Will the fight still bring in a million bucks? Will the extra twenty-four hours help or hurt the Brown Bomber?

Joe spent the extra time eating, sleeping, and relaxing. In a matter of hours, he'd be fighting an over-the-hill ex-champ for a third of a million dollars. And, once he got past Schmeling, he'd challenge Braddock for the title.

Things were lining up beautifully.

June 19, 1936

The rain had stopped, and at ten o'clock a cool breeze was blowing across the field in Yankee Stadium. A boxing ring, lit by a bank of lights overhead, took up the area around second base. Joe sat on his stool, waiting for the opening bell. Schmeling sat upright in the opposite corner. The tuxedoed ring announcer, Harry Balogh, stepped into the center of the ring and took hold of the microphone that dropped down from the scaffold.

"Fifteen rounds," Balogh declared, his voice echoing through the stadium public address system. "Wearing purple trunks, 192, former heavyweight champion, coming back in the role of a challenger for heavyweight honors, Max Schmeling."

The crowd cheered, and Schmeling got off his stool and raised his gloves. Then the seventy thousand spectators quieted down in anticipation of Joe's name.

"And his very capable opponent," Balogh said in a booming voice, "wearing black trunks, 198, one of the greatest heavyweights in the annals of fistiana, *Joe Louis!*"

A deafening roar rose from deep within all three tiers

of the massive stadium. Joe stood up and acknowledged the crowd. Then he looked across the ring and sized up Schmeling. The ex-champ looked to be in superb shape, but Joe knew better. Schmeling was older, slower, and less powerful than the men Joe had become accustomed to fighting.

When the bell rang, Joe circled his target, looking for an opening. Schmeling had an awkward, crouching style. He left his body unguarded—his long left arm sticking out, his right arm cocked—but it was tough to land a solid shot. Joe shifted strategies, jabbing with his left, picking at Schmeling, keeping him at bay.

It seemed as if both fighters were playing a game of cat and mouse and that it was just a matter of time before Joe figured out the German's style. But in the middle of the fourth round, Schmeling uncorked an overhand right that connected squarely with Joe's left temple. Joe recovered, but got the message: *You're in for a fight tonight.*

"I knew then that not only was it hard for me to hit Schmeling," Joe said, "but that he seemed to know when to hit me, and hurt me."

It was bound to happen again, and it did. After a rapid left-right combination, Schmeling landed another, and another. Joe hadn't seen them coming, and before he realized what was happening, he was bouncing on the canvas, engulfed by screams from the shocked crowd.

The first right "hit me like a bolt of lightning. I saw stars, and they weren't the kind above the stadium," Joe said. "Then another right came. . . . It landed on my jaw. I turned in a daze and sank to the canvas."

Joe was back on his feet in a flash, but his head was still a second behind. This couldn't be happening. He was the one who knocked opponents to their butts; he wasn't supposed to land on his, and certainly not at the hands of a has-been like Schmeling. When the round ended, Joe shuffled to his corner and collapsed on his stool, tired, dazed, and ashamed.

"Didn't I tell you to watch that right?" Chappie said. "Go back in there and keep your guard up higher. Keep

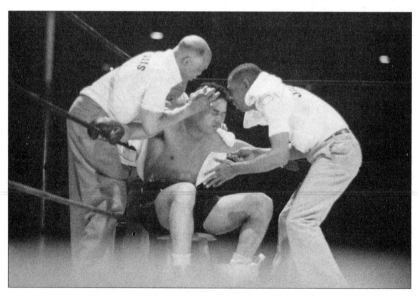

Continually urging their fighter to block Max's right, Chappie Blackburn (left) and assistant Larry Amadee work on Joe before the twelfth round.

jabbin' hard with your left, and when you get an opening, cross with your right."

It was a sound plan, and Joe nodded and went back out to battle. But Chappie's instructions would only work if Joe could see that right hand coming. Schmeling kept it hidden behind his rib cage and seemed to launch it from somewhere in the outfield bleachers.

Within seconds, Joe got hit again. And again. It was the same punch—that damned, explosive, overhand right—and he couldn't avoid it. Finally, in the twelfth round, after spending the whole night trying in vain to duck that cinderblock of a fist, Joe took a battering like no other.

Clem McCarthy called the fight on NBC radio:

> *Schmeling stepped back and shot a hard right hand to Louis's jaw that landed flush and made Louis step into a clinch. And Donovan* [the referee] *broke them. Schmeling got over two more hard rights to Louis's jaw, and made Louis give ground. And there, Schmeling straightened up Louis with hard rights and lefts to the jaw. He has puffed up Louis's left cheek and Louis is down! Louis is down! Hanging to the ropes, hanging badly. He is a very tired fighter. He is blinking his eyes, shaking his head. The count is done. The fight is over. The fight is over. And Schmeling is the winner! Louis is completely out!*

Having failed to block Schmeling's right, Joe lies on the canvas as referee Arthur Donovan counts him out and Schmeling celebrates.

Joe rolled over on the canvas. The ring was spinning—the whole damned stadium was spinning—and Joe, face down, shook his head, hoping, somehow, to rattle the nausea, weakness, confusion, and shame out of his head. What just happened? How did it happen? Had he really lost?

Veteran newspaperman Grantland Rice sat ringside hammering at his typewriter keys. The Teletype sent his words to papers around the country. "The atom has been taken apart," he wrote. "The myth of the superman has been exploded completely."

Nobody knew it more than Joe Louis.

"I done everything wrong," he said.

The Helpless Giant

Joe was slumped in a chair in his dressing room, his face stinging, his eyes swollen, and his straw hat sitting crookedly on his throbbing head. He had showered and changed back into his gray suit. He didn't want to hear his handlers remind him that he had spent too much time on the golf course and not enough time training. And he was too embarrassed to face the horde of reporters trying to squeeze through the door, desperate for a quote.

Chappie did the talking for him. "He got tagged, that's all," he told the press. "Yep, Schmeling hit him with a short right in the fourth round from which Joe never recovered. Maybe it's best that Joe got knocked out. Everything was coming too easy for him."

When the door shut and Joe was alone with Chappie, he let out a stream of heart-wrenching sobs, the kind of cries he hadn't heard come out of his chest since he was a little boy. He dried his eyes with a handkerchief, trying to accept that he'd not only lost to Schmeling, but had also blown his shot at the title.

Adding to Joe's despair was the failing health of his stepfather, Pat Brooks. Just before the fight, Brooks had suffered a stroke and was laid up at home in Detroit, too sick to listen to the broadcast. (He would die a few weeks later, never knowing Joe had lost.)

"He thought I could beat anybody in the world," Joe

said. "I wanted him to have something real good out of my fighting, because of the good things he did for us Barrows." Joe had poured a chunk of his boxing riches into the family, but the money had never mattered to Brooks. He continued working as a street sweeper for the Department of Public Works until he was too sick to lift the broom.

It was time for Joe to leave the stadium, and for the first time in twenty-five professional fights, he would do so on the losing end.

James T. Farrell described Joe's departure in the *Nation* magazine. "Photographers stood on chairs, awaiting Louis's exit, begging for just one picture," he wrote. "Louis sat, still punch drunk. He went out like a drunken man, surrounded by cops and members of his retinue, his face hidden behind a straw hat and the collar of his gray topcoat. Unsupported, he would have fallen. The helpless giant was pushed into a taxicab and hustled away while a crowd fought with the police to obtain a glance at him."

Joe wasn't the only one struggling with the sudden turn of events. He'd been a king to black America, and his followers couldn't bear seeing him dethroned.

One Harlem resident, the poet Langston Hughes, attended the fight. "I walked down Seventh Avenue and saw grown men weeping like children, and women sitting on the curbs with their heads in their hands," he wrote afterward. "All across the country that night when the news came that Joe was knocked out, people cried."

Wendell Smith, a sportswriter for the black-owned *Pittsburgh Courier*, put his readers' pain into words. "You have seen a man down limp and useless, his eyes glassy and swollen. You have seen the rich blood of your idol flowing from his nose, mouth and cuts about the face. . . . You have seen the perfect fighting machine, Joe Louis, beaten by a grim, determined German . . . Max Schmeling. You will never forget the things you have seen. Never, as long as you live . . . will you forget."

Journalists in the South, where Jim Crow laws were still the norm, had a different reaction. These white writers, the same ones who had praised Joe as the ideal boxer, now turned on him. They called him a sham and a second-class citizen and denounced him as an uneducated black man, a no-brains buffoon who'd been outmaneuvered by a smarter, white fighter. America, they said, had been saved from its darkest nightmare: a black heavyweight champion.

Even in the halls of Washington, some congressmen representing southern states—Joe's birthplace—celebrated his defeat. They were so jubilant when the fight ended that they brought all business to a standstill. As the *Atlanta Constitution* reported, "Cheers for Max Schmeling's startling knockout of Joe Louis stopped transaction of important business in congress for several minutes tonight. Many members of the house who had slipped out to listen to the fight on their office radios surged back onto the floor

in a rousing demonstration after the knockout. Similar dis-
order occurred in the staid senate chamber."

William McG. Keefe of the New Orleans *Times-Picayune*
penned an article saying that boxing's reign of terror had
ended. "The big bad wolf has been chased from the door,"
he wrote.

Joe's dream of fighting for the championship was
over. The only thing he could do to prove the hate-mongers
wrong—to show them that he was as smart, as strong, and
as capable as any white fighter—was to beat Max Schmeling should they ever meet again.

CHAPTER 6

Meeting with Hitler

Max peered out the window of the *Hindenburg*. The airship, an 800-foot-long, hydrogen-filled torpedo with swastikas plastered on its tail fins, was descending into the Frankfurt airport. A fleet of German air force planes escorted it as it touched down.

When Max stepped onto the promenade deck, swarms of onlookers cheered the returning hero. He straightened his back, stood stiffly upright, and to the delight of the jam-packed crowd, thrust out his right arm in a Nazi salute. It felt good to be back in Germany, and even better to be back in the limelight.

Max was feted again the next day when he was the guest of honor at the Reich Chancellery. He had donned his sharpest suit, shaved his stubbly cheeks, and together with his wife, Anny, his mother, Amanda, and a few friends, boarded one of Hitler's private planes for the

Germans salute Max upon his arrival in Frankfurt.

flight to Berlin. There, he was greeted with an honor guard of five hundred amateur boxers dressed in blue boxing tights.

At the Chancellery, a group of welcoming guards led Max and his party into the reception hall, where Hitler was waiting, dressed in a double-breasted gray suit.

"On behalf of all of Germany, I congratulate you," the führer said, vigorously shaking Max's hand.

Hitler then motioned for his guests to enter a large dining room and instructed each person on where to sit. As cake and coffee were served, he bombarded Max with questions about the fight, demanding details of every round. Max reached into his bag, took out a stack of press clippings, and passed them around. The führer marveled at the images, zeroing in on the ones of Max raising his arms in victory.

"Simply terrific," he said. "Boxing is a manly sport. That's why I tell everyone that it should be introduced into the public school curriculum."

Hitler then moved everyone into a screening room to watch the films of the fight, which had just arrived through customs. When the projector started whirring and the black-and-white images of Yankee Stadium flickered to life on the screen, Hitler leaned forward, intent on catching every frame.

For Max, it was a pleasure to relive his triumphant night. There he was in all his glory, his muscles bulging and his punches strong, especially that sweet right hand that couldn't miss. As he had hinted to the press, he'd found a hole in Louis's defense. In his recent fights, Louis had been unconsciously making the rookie mistake of dropping his left hand after throwing a jab, and Max had plowed through that opening again and again. Defeating the Brown Bomber had been even easier than expected. And now, against all odds, here he was, the toast of Germany, sitting with the führer, on his way to fighting Braddock and reclaiming the championship.

Watching the fourth round, when Louis fell to the canvas, Hitler slapped his thigh with delight. "What a specimen," he said, turning and beaming at Max.

Max at the Reich Chancellery. Hitler beams as he reads of Max's victory over Joe Louis.

At the end of the screening, Hitler ordered his propaganda minister, Joseph Goebbels, to turn the fight into a documentary film.

"Goebbels," he said, practically shouting, "this film must be shown as a main feature throughout the Third Reich!"

Goebbels followed orders, and within days the documentary *Max Schmeling's Victory—a German Victory* was playing in movie theaters across the country.

An assistant turned on the lights and the führer stood up.

"Thank you for coming," he said to the gathering. "Now it's time to leave."

It was an abrupt departure, but Max left with his chest out. He'd come to admire Hitler—he even kept a signed photo of him in his study at home. He enjoyed having the führer flatter him in front of his friends and family, telling him he was as fine an Aryan specimen as the world had ever seen.

The same day he met with Hitler, the Nazi newspaper *Der Angriff* ran an interview with Max, praising him for proving white supremacy. "Schmeling, the German, did that for the Americans," the article read, "the same people who did not want to give him a chance, who mocked him, derided him. He succeeded against world opinion. And he says he would not have had the strength if he had not known what support he had in his homeland."

Another Nazi publication, the weekly *Das Schwarze Korps*, boasted that "Schmeling's victory was not only sport. It was a question of prestige for our race."

Max certainly seemed to be enjoying the benefits of Nazi patronage. He was becoming the center of attention at movie premieres, galas, and black-tie dinners. Fellow Germans surrounded him, excited to meet Max Schmeling, the Aryan god. Although he wasn't an official member of the Nazi party, Max never used his time in the spotlight to renounce it, either.

Six weeks after his visit with Hitler, Max was back in Berlin to attend the 1936 Summer Olympics. The Nazi government had spent the past few years polishing the city, fixing up dilapidated buildings, repaving streets and sidewalks, building new boulevards, even constructing a new subway line. Hitler, well aware that the world would be watching, also set out to disprove the notion that Berlin had become a center of racism and oppression and ordered the removal of all Nazi propaganda. Placards posted around the city stating NO JEWS ALLOWED were ripped down. Anti-Semitic newspapers also vanished, replaced by works of literature banned by the Nazi regime. To Max's delight, a bronze statue of his own likeness— complete with sculpted muscles and a narrow, tight waist—was on display outside the Olympic Stadium.

More than 110,000 spectators came out for the opening ceremonies, and Max was paraded across the complex, surrounded by throngs of admiring athletes and coaches. In the Olympic Village, when he spotted Jesse Owens, the American track and field star from Ohio State University, Max grabbed the black man's hand and shook it with great flourish.

"I've heard lots about you," Max said, in open admiration. He didn't appear to share Hitler's condemnation of blacks as an inferior race. In fact, he told Owens that he expected to see great things from him.

Soon after visiting the Olympic Village, Max made a speedy return to New York on the *Hindenburg*. He was asked what he thought of the American Olympians— especially Owens, who wound up winning four gold

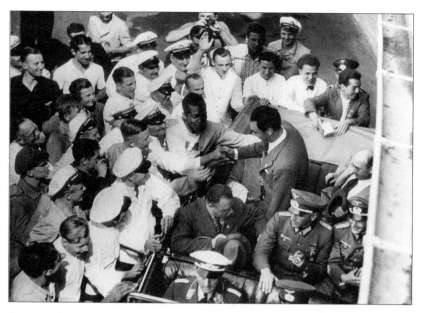

Fans in the Olympic Village clamor around Max in August 1936.

medals. "They are great," Max said. "Mr. Owens is the most perfect athlete I have ever seen. He flies like the *Hindenburg*."

Max was in training for his title shot against Braddock. But every time the fight was planned, something got in the way. Braddock injured his finger. Braddock needed more time. Braddock had a problem with the contract.

But the truth wasn't nearly as random. Despite Hitler's efforts to hide his actions, reports of Nazi persecution had made their way to America. Plus, word had spread that Hitler snubbed Jesse Owens by storming out of the Olympic stadium after Owens took his fourth gold medal. That anti-Nazi sentiment had zeroed in on Max.

Jewish groups were already threatening to boycott his fights, and nobody in the boxing business wanted any part of a Braddock-Schmeling match. Even though Braddock had taken the belt in a stunning upset over Max Baer, the general consensus was that he was shot as a fighter. He'd won only fifteen of his last thirty-eight fights. As promoters saw it, putting Max in the ring with such an easy mark was the same as handing the Nazis the title.

It didn't matter whether Max was officially a Nazi; he was as tied to the party as any of Hitler's other henchmen. He hadn't spoken out against the führer or said a word about the Nazis' racist ideology or persecution of Jews. And so, while Max was adored in Germany, he was reviled by the rest of the world.

"I Won't Let My People Down"

They're called backroom deals because they happen when nobody is looking, in places where there aren't any rules. And in 1937, it was a backroom deal that determined the fate of the world heavyweight championship. It happened at the Twentieth Century Sporting Club in Manhattan, in the office of Joe Louis's promoter Mike Jacobs—the boxing kingpin who put together most every heavyweight title match.

Braddock's manager, Joe Gould, approached the promoter with a deal: Braddock would agree to fight Louis instead of Schmeling if Braddock could have 10 percent of the money Jacobs made from every heavyweight championship fight he promoted over the next decade. By making this offer, Gould was breaking the most sacred code of honor in the sport—he was selling a shot at the title. But Mike Jacobs feared Joe would never get another shot if Schmeling won the title and took it to Germany. He accepted the deal.

So, in the end, it was that simple. On a handshake, and the promise of ten years of free money, Schmeling was out, and Louis was in—and on the verge of becoming the first black champion since Jack Johnson lost the belt twenty-two years earlier.

The Braddock-Louis fight was set for June 22, 1937, and Joe got right to work. He wasn't about to embarrass himself the way he had against Schmeling. After that debacle, he'd won his next seven fights, six by knockout, but still felt he had something to prove. If he could beat Braddock and win the title, he would somewhat redeem himself—and his entire race. As he told William Nunn of the *Pittsburgh Courier*, "I won't let my people down."

Joe set up camp in Kenosha, Wisconsin, seventy miles from Chicago, the site of the match. Under Chappie's supervision, he woke up every morning at five o'clock, ran ten miles, went back to his cottage and slept until ten, and then ate a breakfast of orange juice, prunes, and meat, usually liver or lamb chops. In the early afternoon, he hit the heavy bag, went through a series of stretching exercises, and sparred in an outdoor gym. At five in the afternoon, he ate a dinner of meat and fresh fish, vegetables, and ice cream. By nine, he was in bed with the lights out.

On the day of the fight, with a cool summer breeze blowing through Chicago, sixty-five thousand spectators, nearly half of them black, made their way through the turnstiles at Comiskey Park. Special trains and planes had brought spectators from all over the country. Five hundred reporters were on hand to cover the fight, and more than a hundred radio stations—in Australia, Asia, Africa, Europe, and South America—were set to broadcast it.

Joe was only twenty-three. If he beat Braddock, he would become the youngest heavyweight champion in history. But he was so highly regarded, and Braddock so dismissed, that he was a 2-1 favorite. When the bell rang, he left his corner and approached the champion, bouncing on the balls of his feet, bobbing, weaving, and looking for an opening. Braddock stood straight up and moved slowly, providing a ready target. Joe remained cautious. Braddock was getting older, but nothing was certain. This was the same fighter who had upset Max Baer to take the title.

In the first round, Joe threw a combination, and Braddock responded with a one-two punch of his own, but he missed his mark, no doubt rusty from a two-year layoff. The fighters exchanged a few more flurries, flashy but mostly harmless, until Braddock uncorked a blistering right uppercut that nailed Joe squarely on the chin. The next thing Joe knew, he was on the canvas.

Could this really be happening again?

Joe bounced right up, determined to prove that he could take a punch, that he had a champion's heart. Braddock rushed at him, throwing punches at his head, viciously and wildly, hoping to end the fight with one more monstrous blow. But Joe ducked and dodged, managing to stave off danger until the bell rang.

Once the second round got going, Joe's head cleared, and he started to find his rhythm. His timing was sharper, his punches crisper, his reflexes quicker. He launched sizzling rockets at Braddock, but the champion set off a few of his own, and both fighters were soon tired and bloodied. In the fifth round, Joe seemed to gain strength. He hammered Braddock repeatedly, but the champ refused to go down. Two rounds later, Joe tagged him again, pummeling him with combinations, but the champ, his lip cut, his gloves heavy, still wouldn't fall. In the eighth, Joe landed a whizzing left to the ribs and a picture-perfect right to the jaw. Braddock dropped like a pair of unbuckled trousers, and lay on the canvas, facedown and motionless, as the referee stood over him, counting.

There wasn't a soul in the crowd who thought Braddock would get up after being hit like that. He himself said, "I couldn't have got up if they'd offered me a million dollars."

When the count hit ten, it was over. Joe had just won the world heavyweight title. Flashbulbs popped, Joe's handlers mobbed the ring, and well-wishers followed. The crowd showered the new heavyweight champion with thunderous cheers, and Chappie kissed the glove on Joe's right hand.

"Ol' glove," he shouted, "you sure had dynamite in you tonight!"

No one was more impressed with Joe's power than the man he defeated. "His jab," Braddock said, "was like someone jammed an electric light in your face and busted it."

Joe celebrates with Jack "Chappie" Blackburn (holding boxing glove). John Roxborough is behind Blackburn, and comanager Julian Black is to Joe's left.

In black communities across America, spontaneous victory parades broke out. But Joe himself wasn't ready to rejoice. He felt a bit like an imposter, a guy who'd snuck his way to the title. He didn't deserve the accolades. Not yet, anyway.

"I don't want nobody to call me champ until I beat Max Schmeling," he said. "Bring on Max Schmeling. Bring him on."

CHAPTER 7

Public Enemy No. 1

Max was still itching for a shot at the title. Sure, Louis would be tougher to defeat than Braddock, but what did it matter? Max had already beaten the Brown Bomber—badly. If given the opportunity, he'd do it again. Besides, Max wasn't getting any younger. He was thirty-two. Time was running out.

The good news was that Louis couldn't wait to get another crack at Max. So, in September 1937, only three months after the Brown Bomber took the title from Braddock, the deal was done. The rematch would take place on June 22, 1938. Max would earn 20 percent of the gate, an estimated $200,000—half of what Louis was promised.

"I do not mind making concessions, so long as I am sure I will have the chance to win back the title," Max told the press. "I am a businessman, too, but the money is secondary, in this case."

By the time Max signed the contract, the political winds drifting into America from Germany had erupted into a full-blown tornado. Hitler had joined forces with Italy's dictator, Benito Mussolini, and Japan's emperor, Hirohito, and the threesome had begun spreading terror throughout Europe and Asia.

American newspapers screamed headlines about the spread of Nazi tyranny.

JEWS DISAPPEAR FROM STREETS
AS VIENNA SEETHES
—*Chicago Daily Tribune*

ALARMED WORLD WATCHES HITLER
IN NEW NAZI CRISIS
—*Atlanta Constitution*

5,000,000 JEWS WARNED TO QUIT AUSTRIA
—*Boston Globe*

HITLER STRIKES AGAIN
—*New York Times*

AUSTRIA OPENS ANTI-SEMITIC CAMPAIGN
—*Los Angeles Times*

So in the spring of 1938, when Max arrived in New York to prepare for the fight, he was public enemy number one. When he stepped off the SS *Bremen*, picketers shouted his name and mocked his status as an Aryan superman. They held signs that read, DON'T LET MAX

SCHMELING TAKE AMERICAN MONEY BACK TO NAZI GERMANY and SCHMELING IS A CITIZEN OF NAZI GERMANY. He found another group of protesters waiting at his hotel, the Essex House. He passed without incident—only to arrive at his suite and face a roomful of reporters. There, in a burst of 1930s trash talk, he told the *Pittsburgh Courier* that he had a "strong psychological superiority" over Louis, and that even though he was getting older, age wasn't slowing him down. "I intend to become his ringmaster," he said. "I have been fighting for 14 years and know all the tricks of the game."

Max was no fool. It was obvious that the New York State Athletic Commission expected—even wanted—him to lose. But all he had to do was hammer Louis with his magical right hand. If he could do that again, it would be an early night.

Anti-Nazi League protesters make it clear how they feel about Max.

He headed upstate to his training camp in the Adirondacks and took on a punishing schedule of jogging, sparring, and calisthenics. In the evenings, he relaxed in the quiet surroundings, content to sit alone for hours on the porch of his cabin. When reporters visited, he spoke eagerly of his conditioning, insisting he had the stamina of a twenty-five-year-old.

"I crossed the Atlantic eight times . . . traveled 55,500 miles . . . waited two years for this second crack at Louis,. You don't think I'm going to lose now, do you?" he told the press. "They tell me that the poor Negro boy is worried. Of course he's worried. He'll never get over what I gave him in our first fight. Fighters just don't recover from beatings like that."

Max oozed confidence. He was in great shape, looked sharp in training, and predicted that he'd have no trouble at Yankee Stadium come June.

Nobody had any reason to doubt him.

Except that his opponent was saying the same thing.

"Snus"

It was only natural that with Hitler's actions in Europe, American journalists would amp up the political implications of the fight. The battle soon grew into much more than a contest between two prizefighters. It became democracy against fascism. Roosevelt against Hitler. Had you asked almost any American, you'd have heard that Joe Louis was taking on the führer himself.

William Jones of Baltimore's *Afro-American* reported it this way: "Not only in Germany is the political tension high, but in France and Czechoslovakia, where there is widespread hope that Louis will win. Never before in history, it is stated, has a prizefight been likely to play so great a part in world affairs, outside of the sporting field, as the Louis-Schmeling bout."

United Press sports columnist Henry McLemore shared the same sentiment: "Not since the barbed-wire bearded Dempsey and the cunning, cutting Tunney came to grips in Chicago has New York, the United States, and the world been so excited by a prizefight. . . . It is international, pitting a foreigner against a native, and the fact that the foreigner is a German, a Nazi, fighting in the world's largest Jewish city, has not hurt the sale of tickets."

In the eye of the storm was Pompton Lakes, New Jersey—the site of Joe's training camp. During the week, swarms of journalists showed up, trailing the champion for news on his schedule, his workouts, anything fit to print. On the weekend, thousands of celebrities, fans, and curiosity seekers—many from states as far away as California, Texas, and Florida—paid $1.10 to watch Joe get in shape. When there were no seats left, men in linen suits and women in cotton dresses perched themselves in trees, atop automobiles, and on fences and nearby roof-tops. The champ lived up to expectations. In sparring sessions, he cut down his opponents with superhuman precision. And when he strolled the grounds, flanked by two cops and a bodyguard, he gave off the same godlike quality that he projected in the ring.

Babe Ruth came to visit him. So did Jesse Owens. Joe DiMaggio, Duke Ellington, and Bill "Bojangles" Robinson also came by. All of them told Joe the same thing: *You gotta beat this guy.*

Joe prepares for a sparring session in Pompton Lakes before the Schmeling rematch.

Privately, Joe had his own score to settle. Yes, he longed to undo his loss to Schmeling. But he also wanted to avenge Hitler's callous treatment of his friend Jesse Owens at the Berlin Olympics. He was furious when he heard that Hitler had walked out on the black medalist after his Olympic victory. Joe was proud of Owens for having upstaged Hitler and the Nazis with his performance, and he couldn't wait to do the same against Schmeling.

The Brown Bomber wasn't the only one who wanted to see Hitler crushed. Joe even had the support of millions of white Americans—the same people who had once rooted against him and hoped he wouldn't win the title.

"Schmeling represented everything that Americans disliked," Joe said years later. "They wanted him beat and beat good. Now here I was, a black man. I had the burden of representing all America. . . . White Americans—even while some of them still were lynching black people in the South—were depending on me to K.O. Germany. . . . I knew I had to get Schmeling good. I had my own personal reasons, and the whole damned country was depending on me."

When Joe broke camp, he insisted he was in the best shape of his young career. And he seemed unruffled at the prospect of facing Schmeling again. "Last time I met him I was not an experienced fighter," he told reporters. "I had been winning all my fights just with my strength. Since then I have learned to fight."

Chicago Daily Tribune sportswriter Arch Ward watched Joe's final workouts the day before the fight and declared him fit and ready. Ward assured his readers, "Louis has never been in better condition. Some of his supporters are worrying over the psychological effect of the punishment he took from Schmeling in their last engagement. They are wasting their time. Louis isn't afraid of any man with gloves or without them. It is our guess he will have to be aroused from slumber to go to Yankee Stadium tomorrow night."

Harry Thomas, who fought and lost to both Louis and Schmeling, had no doubt about the outcome. Right after Joe flattened him in April, he said, "I'll bet my purse tonight that Joe will knock the German out. His punches got 'snus.' That's Norwegian for 'umph.'" He went on to add, "He hit me a lot harder than Schmeling did. I think he stretched my neck a foot when he clouted me in the third round."

Jimmy Cannon, of the *New York Journal and American*, who had predicted Schmeling's victory the first time around, told Joe, "I'm betting a knockout in six rounds."

Joe looked at Cannon, shook his head, and held up a single finger.

"It goes one," he said.

The Big Night

When June 22 rolled around, the eyes of the world were fixed on Yankee Stadium. Earlier in the day, extra-long trains rolled into Pennsylvania Station from Chicago, Cleveland, Detroit, Cincinnati, St. Louis, and

Washington, D.C. Transatlantic ships arrived at the New York harbor carrying two thousand wealthy Germans.

Ringside seats had been selling for an eye-popping hundred bucks, but that didn't stop crowds of people from descending on the Twentieth Century Sporting Club in midtown Manhattan, hoping to nab last-minute tickets.

Three thousand extra police officers patrolled the city, a third of them dispatched to Harlem. There, massive traffic jams slowed cars and taxis to a crawl as they made their way along the avenues. Crowds of chanting pedestrians walked past police horses and local shops holding signs that read, WELCOME, JOE LOUIS FANS.

Up in the Bronx, the rain that had been falling throughout the day had stopped, and the air in Yankee Stadium was thick, muggy, and hot. As the sun began to set and the overhead lights fired up, the ticket-sellers shuttered their booths. All seats were sold. Managers at movie theaters, dance clubs, even wrestling matches, interrupted their events so patrons could gather around radios. Harlem had descended into an eerie silence. The same was true for cities and towns around the country, nowhere more so than Joe's adopted home of Chicago.

Jersey Joe Walcott, a black fighter who would go on to win the world heavyweight championship in 1951, looked out his window in Camden, New Jersey, and saw only deserted streets. "Everyone was inside listening to the fight on the radio," he said.

Near Plains, Georgia, thirteen-year-old Jimmy Carter, the future president of the United States, sat in the living room of his family's farmhouse. Like most of the rural South at the time, the Carters didn't have electricity, but they had a large battery-powered radio. A few of the family's black neighbors, not having radios of their own, had asked Jimmy's father, Earl, if they could come by and listen to the fight. When more than forty showed up, he placed the radio on the ledge of the front window. The neighbors fanned out under a mulberry tree and waited quietly for the sound of announcer Clem McCarthy's voice.

In Germany, where it was the middle of the night, twenty million residents sat awake in bedrooms, living rooms, and kitchens, their radios crackling, their hearts pounding.

In a small dressing room under the stands in Yankee Stadium, Max threw light punches in the air, trying to stay calm. His manager and friend, Joe Jacobs, wasn't by his side this time; he was listening at home, having been suspended for his ties to another boxer. Max had never felt more alone.

Joe shadowboxed in his own dressing room for a half hour, much longer than his usual ten minutes.

Mike Jacobs, the promoter who'd made the backroom deal to get Joe his title shot, came in and gave him a pep talk. "Murder that bum," he said. "And don't make a sucker out of me."

It was two minutes before ten o'clock when Joe finally headed down the runway. He was dressed in his familiar blue silk robe, the one with JOE LOUIS stitched on the back. As he stepped out of the third-base dugout, the crowd erupted into a resounding cheer that said, *You're our savior*, as clearly as it did, *Kill that Nazi bastard*.

Joe made his way past the pitcher's mound to the ring, flanked by handlers, bodyguards, and security personnel, politely shaking hands as the din continued.

Max followed minutes later. The instant he planted his German foot on the American baseball field, the booing began. It was the sound of fear, of hatred, of eighty thousand barking pit bulls. Cigarette butts flew down from the upper decks, as did used banana peels and crumpled paper cups. Max draped a towel over his head and, with twenty-five police officers acting as escorts, tossed a few jabs in the air as he bounced his way to the ring, nodding and looking out at the crowd with a faint smile.

CHAPTER 8

The Fight

The booing continued as Max climbed into the ring and walked over to Joe, who was facing the crowd. Max tapped him on the shoulder and, when Joe turned around, extended his right glove.

Joe, shutting out the noise around him, nodded and shook Max's hand, then patted him on the shoulder before turning away again.

Max went back to his corner, and the ring announcer, Harry Balogh, wearing his trademark tuxedo, stepped to the center of the canvas. Holding a sheet of paper in his hand, he took the microphone.

"Fifteen rounds for the world's heavyweight championship," he bellowed, revving the stadium's wattage into the red zone. "Weighing 193, wearing purple trunks, outstanding contender for heavyweight honors, the former heavyweight titleholder, Max Schmeling."

Max got off his stool and bowed, his patterned robe draped over his shoulders. The crowd reacted with a rumbling of cheers and jeers.

"Weighing 198 and three-quarters," Balogh continued, "wearing black trunks, the famous Detroit Brown Bomber, world's heavyweight champion, Joe Louis."

The champ stepped forward to a thunderous roar; then he circled back to his corner and threw some light punches.

The referee, Arthur Donovan, called the two fighters to the center of the ring and went through his usual prefight drill, telling the combatants to keep it clean.

Max trained his eyes on Joe, trying to ignore the bloodthirsty Americans staring down at him. Joe wore a poker face, not letting on that he was itching to get started, that adrenaline was busting out of his pores.

"I felt like a racehorse at the gate," he said. "I was rarin' to go."

Donovan finished his instructions, ordered the fighters to their corners, and finally, after months of fanfare, hype, and political propaganda, the bell rang. And when it did, seventy million people around the world leaned toward their radios, listening to broadcasts in English, German, Spanish, and Portuguese.

In America, NBC announcer Clem McCarthy described the scene in his customary rapid-fire delivery:

And Joe Louis is in the center of the ring. Max circling around him. Joe Louis lets go with two straight lefts to the chin—both of them light stuff. As the men clinch. Joe Louis tries to get over two hard lefts and Max ties him up and they break away clean. On the far side of the ring now, Max with his back to the ropes and Louis hooks a left to Max's head quickly, and shoots over a hard right to Max's head. Louis, a left to Max's jaw, a right to his head. Max shoots a hard right to Louis, and Louis with the old one-two, first the left and then the right.

Joe had no intention of letting up, no thoughts of pacing himself. "I knew my whole career depended on this," he said. "It was going to be all or nothing."

He fired a left. Then a right. Then an uppercut. Then a left-right combination. They were fast and hard, and they all connected squarely.

Max tried to get away, to cover himself, to run, but he was being showered in leather. He backed up, stumbled, and, as he tried to regain his balance, took a vicious right to the jaw. He bounced back to the ropes and covered up again. Joe's punches rained down, smashing Max's head, striking his jaw, whipping his neck. A left slammed into Max's gut, and he let out a high-pitched cry, an agonizing, distant, pleading voice that he himself didn't recognize. He needed to think, to figure out what the hell was happening, but the assault kept coming, missiles colliding with his head and body. *Bam. Bam. Bam.* Again. Again. Again. His knees buckled, and he clutched the ropes, grateful he was still on his feet, but fearful that he had fourteen more rounds to endure.

Donovan separated the fighters, and Max looked to his corner for help. His trainer Max Machon shouted instructions—uncork the right, block his cross, bob, weave—but Max couldn't, not while defending against a

Max tumbles to the canvas in this photo from the Associated Press.

fusillade of punches. He wanted his head to clear; he wanted the bell to ring. He stepped forward and got nailed with a two-punch combination that he wasn't quick enough to block, a pair of picture-perfect bull's-eyes, one to the jaw and a follow-up to the temple. He tumbled at Joe's feet, his mind screaming to get up, to fight like a champion.

He couldn't let it end, not like this, not on the canvas, not in front of so many scornful Americans, not with his countrymen listening in horror. He rolled over and got to his feet, but his legs crumbled, his bones melted, his soul drained. The crowd noise, now a distant clamor, had given way to an incessant buzz coming from deep within his ears.

Joe knew Max was shot, as did everyone in the stadium. So when Max got up, Joe rushed in, discarding any notions of defense, any fear of Max's right hand. He threw a barrage of punches, and Max fell a second time, face first, both of his gloved hands smacking the canvas.

German radio announcer Arno Helmis, sitting ringside, described the action back to his homeland in near hysteria: "Schmeling gives in the knees. . . . Maxie goes to the floor! . . . Maxie! Maxie! For God's sake! . . . Schmeling is up again, he stands—Maxxxxie!"

Max's instinct was to fight, but his brain wasn't firing, and Joe let loose with another battery of punches. Max took a whizzing left-left-right to the head—*bam, bam, pow!*—and went down again. When he tried to climb to his feet, his limbs were too rubbery. He felt as though he were crawling on a mat of hot, gooey taffy. Machon threw a towel into the ring, signaling that his fighter was quitting, but the referee Donovan ignored the gesture. He picked up the towel, threw it on the ropes, and started counting over the fallen man.

Two, three, four . . .

It was clear Max wasn't going to beat the count, not even if it went to a hundred. Machon raced into the ring to save his fighter. All that was left was the official announcement, and it came when Donovan waved his hands in the air. After only two minutes and four seconds, Joe Louis had knocked out Max Schmeling, and in the eyes of America, all of Nazi Germany.

His voice all but gone, Helmis assured his listeners in Germany, "I will still say to the blonde little wife in Berlin that Maxie [is] standing up. His eye is not cut open and his face is not ruined." The line went dead, presumably because officials in Germany didn't like the outcome of the fight.

The crowd went into a frenzy, letting out a mighty cheer that was matched in living rooms, bars, and restaurants across America. Fans pounded one another's backs; writers in press row smacked their typewriters and jumped out of their seats; strangers hugged and kissed— all of them bonded by the thrill of Joe's victory. Even some of the onlookers who had applauded Max before the fight got caught up in the excitement and were chanting Joe's name.

Max's cornermen led their fighter back to his stool—his head down, his body busted, broken, nauseous, aching—as Joe and his handlers celebrated across the ring. Harry Balogh took the microphone and declared Joe the winner, giving him the spotlight that Max had always craved.

Leaning on Machon, Max pulled himself to his feet and stumbled across the ring. His arms felt as heavy as a pair of rusty water pipes, but he lifted them high enough to grab hold of Joe's shoulders.

"You're a real champion," he said, before being dragged back to his stool, where he wept into his sweat towel.

Half an hour later, sitting in his dressing room, semiconscious, Max tried to regain his pride by telling reporters that his moment of glory was still coming.

"He has beat me," he said, "but I will fight him again."

Meanwhile, reporters, fans, and celebrities trooped into Joe's dressing room like a colony of ants attacking spilled honey. A battery of uniformed police officers, guarding the entrance, made room for New York Mayor Fiorello La Guardia, who entered with a broad smile on his face and his finger wagging in the air. La Guardia, who stood five-two, reached up and gave the still-sweaty Joe a hug, thanking him for winning and sticking it to Germany.

In Harlem, ecstatic residents burst out of their apartments onto the street, cheering, chanting, and singing. Women danced; men swigged from bottles and passed them on to strangers. Bands sprang up, performing on street corners. Shoeshine boys cried, "Get your Joe Louis shine, [only] two minutes and four seconds"—the same amount of time it took Joe to prove his supremacy in the ring.

"A hundred thousand black people surged out of taprooms, flats, restaurants, and filled the streets and sidewalks like the Mississippi River overflowing in flood time," wrote author Richard Wright. "With their faces to the night sky, they filled their lungs with air and let out a scream of

Blacks celebrate Joe's victory in the streets of Harlem.

joy that it seemed would never end, and a scream that seemed to come from untold reserves of strength."

And for one glorious night, the cops didn't mind at all. "This is their night," Police Commissioner Lewis Valentine said. "Let them have their fun."

In Chicago, swing music wafted through the air. The South Side became "a living ocean of smiling faces as crowds flowed out upon the streets," wrote the *Pittsburgh Courier*. "Bands formed, automobiles paraded, dragging old tubs and strings of tin cans behind them. People danced on the sidewalks."

In Philadelphia, Jews and blacks rode together in cars outfitted with homespun noisemakers, presenting a united front for Joe—and against Hitler.

Across the Hudson River in Camden, New Jersey, the deserted streets sprang to life in a series of spontaneous carnivals. "It was like New Year's Eve," said Jersey Joe Walcott.

In Detroit's Black Bottom, a crowd of Joe Louis fans gathered in front of 2100 McDougall Avenue, the home of the champ's mother, Lillie. Ten thousand other residents— many under a banner that read, JOE LOUIS KNOCKED OUT HITLER—celebrated nearby, dancing to Cecil Lee's swing rhythm band.

As the night rolled into the early hours of the morning, the parties migrated from the streets of America's black neighborhoods into bars and nightclubs and private homes.

In the South, black residents, still oppressed despite laying claim to the world heavyweight championship, rejoiced in more subdued tones, careful not to celebrate too loudly.

In Joe's birthplace of LaFayette, Alabama, a gathering of black residents had listened to the fight on a small radio in a black-owned restaurant. "Tense and on edge as the fight began, they were incredulous for several seconds at its sudden ending," the *Pittsburgh Courier* reported. "Then coming suddenly to life they shook hands, exchanged delighted hugs and slaps on the back, filed out and scattered to their respective homes, an occasional whoop marking their progress through the darkened streets."

In rural Georgia, future president Jimmy Carter watched his black neighbors head off for home. "The customs of the South prevailed," he said. "There was not a sound out of the black listeners. Nothing. Just absolute quiet after Louis won. And then they walked across the railroad, a couple hundred yards away, and all hell broke loose. They celebrated all night long, to early, almost daylight, just showing they were proud of Joe Louis."

Even the white southern press—the same newspapers that had treated Joe as a second-class citizen—now put aside its racial biases and grudgingly presented him as an American hero.

Joe and Marva basked in victory at the Harlem apartment of their friend Christopher Savage, a steward on the Pennsylvania Railroad. Joe politely refused the food and champagne that flowed through the apartment and, instead, asked for a bottle of ginger ale and a quart of vanilla ice cream, which he devoured happily.

The day after Joe's triumph, blues musician Bill Gaither recorded a tribute to his boxing hero—one of nearly fifty songs that would be written about Joe over the years. Gaither titled the song, "Champ Joe Louis."

> It was only two minutes and four seconds
> 'Fore Schmeling was down on his knees
> Only two minutes and four seconds
> 'Fore Schmeling was down on his knees
> He looked like he was praying to the good Lord
> To "Have mercy on me, please."

Joe was no longer the black champion. He was America's champion. And after he went to bed, after the pundits published their words, after the musicians sang their songs, it's possible that nobody summed up America's feelings toward Joe more accurately, or more succinctly, than legendary sportswriter Jimmy Cannon:

"He's a credit to his race—the human race."

CHAPTER 9

Max Under Siege

Hospital orderlies wheeled Max out of New York Poly-clinic in the black of night, safe from the prying eyes of photographers and reporters. He'd been admitted ten days earlier, right after the fight with Louis, and been treated for two broken vertebrae. Now, the attendants pushed the busted ex-champion from West 50th Street to Manhattan's West Side piers, where they carried him onboard the SS *Bremen* and wished him safe travels.

Max arrived in Germany a week later. This time around, there were no crowds, no cheers, no planes festooned with swastikas. The only people waiting in Bremerhaven were his wife, Anny, his mother, Amanda, and an underling from the sports minister's office. They helped him down the gangplank and put him on a train to Berlin, where he would spend five more days at a medical clinic.

Having lost to Louis, Max was of little use to the Nazi

regime. His face, which had long been seen on the front page of German newspapers, couldn't even be found in the sports section. The führer no longer invited him to the Chancellery, and German movie directors had no interest in Anny. Films of Max's fights, especially the one showing his loss to Louis, were conspicuously absent from theaters, the reels having been destroyed.

Three months after his defeat, a still-ailing Max showed up at the annual Nazi rally in Nuremberg, just as he always had. Party officials, the same bigwigs who had feted Max at previous events, barely looked his way. After spending years accommodating the führer, attending gatherings, receptions, and rallies, Max was as unwelcome in his own country as he was in America.

"I came home. We were nobody," he said. "It wasn't that Schmeling, the prize fighter, had lost a contest to what the judges and referee called a better man. I had lost for Germany—it was a national calamity." He and Anny were forgotten and left completely alone. "When I lost to the Negro, Joe Louis, our disgrace was complete."

That November, the Nazi regime shifted into overdrive, escalating its hate-mongering into a series of violent attacks throughout Germany, the new Austria, and the German-occupied areas of Czechoslovakia. It was again targeting Jews. Nazi gangs took to the streets, demolishing more than a thousand synagogues and nearly

Although no longer of use to the regime, Max attended the 1938 Nuremberg rally. Here, Hitler heads to the podium.

eight thousand Jewish-owned businesses. They murdered dozens of Jews and arrested thirty thousand more, shuttling them to concentration camps. The event became known as Kristallnacht, which means "night of crystal" but, in this case, referred to the shards of glass littering the streets in the wake of the assaults.

At the time, Max was living in Berlin's Excelsior Hotel. On the first night of the rioting, he returned home to find two teenage boys in the lobby. Max recognized them as Henri and Werner Lewin, the sons of his old Jewish friend David Lewin the owner of the shop where he bought his clothes. Breathless from having run from the mobs during Kristallnacht, the boys said their father had sent them and begged Max to hide them.

Max brought them up to his apartment and told them to stay there, to keep the door locked no matter what they heard going on outside it. Max was breaking the law, and if discovered, he'd be punished as harshly as any anti-Nazi criminal. Still, as the gangs terrorized the streets around him, he kept the boys safe, warm, and well fed. It's unclear why Max took such a risk for the two young men. Whatever the reason, he never discussed it.

"We hid from the housekeepers, waiters, other friends of Max—everyone," Henri Lewin said years later. "The first day, Max didn't leave the apartment. He told the front desk he was sick, and not to let anyone come up. He could have lessened the risk by just telling people we were nephews, or something. But he didn't. He risked everything."

Four days later, after the wave of attacks had subsided, Max sneaked Henri and Werner out of the hotel so the boys could get on a train to Italy.

They didn't make it.

The police seized them and held them in a Berlin prison—only to release them six days later. Miraculously, the boys found their way to Italy, where they were reunited with their father, and the three landed successfully in China and, after the war, the United States.

By now, Max's life, as he knew it, was over. He and Anny moved to the countryside, to a large estate ninety miles northeast of Berlin, close to the border of Poland. Their farmland was adjacent to a nature preserve, and Max could spend his time hunting and relaxing in obscurity.

But late the next summer, Max awoke to a dull roar. Looking out the window, he spotted a squadron of German bombers flying east toward Poland. He ran outside to get a better look and was greeted by one of his farmhands, who, instead of flashing his usual morning smile, said, "Well, Herr Schmeling, this is it. Now it's war."

Sure enough, Hitler had given the order for German troops to invade Poland. On September 3, 1939, France and Britain responded to the invasion by formally declaring war on Germany.

The next year Max was drafted into the German army, despite being thirty-four and well past the traditional age for military service. He was convinced he was being punished for having lost his rematch with Louis. But he had no choice; he had to follow orders. And, in May 1941, he was assigned to the paratroop corps and sent to Greece for the invasion of Crete.

Max parachuted onto the island with his comrades, but his chute didn't open. He landed hard in a vineyard,

Max trains as a paratrooper before Germany's invasion of Crete.

banging up his knee, reinjuring his back, and tangling his feet in vines and parachute strings. He managed to crawl to safety, but spent months recovering from a broken kneecap and a badly injured back.

As for the mission, the Germans succeeded in taking Crete, and the government awarded Max the Iron Cross. But his career in the military was over.

"God's Side"

Joe was an American hero. It was the summer of 1941, and his face could be seen on advertisements for Joe Louis punch, tins of Joe Louis pomade, and bottles of Joe Louis bourbon. Ever since he'd beaten Schmeling, cheering crowds filled arenas wherever he fought. As he swore he would do, he took on all challengers and backed down from no one. In the span of two and half years, he fought thirteen bouts and won them all. He was so dominating, his opponents became known as the Bum of the Month Club.

But just when things were finally going smoothly for Joe, tragedy struck the nation. On December 7, 1941, at eight o'clock in the morning, more than three hundred Japanese fighter planes launched a surprise raid on the United States naval base at Pearl Harbor, in Hawaii. The bombing lasted ninety minutes and killed more than twenty-four hundred Americans, including sixty-eight civilians. The public reacted with horror and fear.

The next day, President Roosevelt went before Congress. He announced, "Yesterday, December 7th, 1941, a date which will live in infamy, the United States of America was suddenly and deliberately attacked by naval and air forces of the Empire of Japan."

The speech lasted only seven minutes, but it instantly galvanized the nation. Within an hour, Congress voted to declare war on Japan.

In twenty-four hours, the world had changed drastically. Americans now turned their attention from the sports section to the front page. Joe was no exception. A month after the attack on Pearl Harbor, he knocked out ring veteran Buddy Baer and donated his $65,200 purse to the Navy Relief Fund.

He also enlisted in the army.

"I knew I'd be glad to help defend America," he said.

"No place else in the world could a onetime black cotton picker like me get to be a millionaire. I love this country like I love my people."

In March 1942, Joe was back at Madison Square Garden, not for a boxing match, but to participate in a rally to raise money for the war effort. Asked to say a few words to the twenty thousand people in the audience, Joe, wearing his private's uniform, walked nervously to the dais and stood behind the microphone.

"I'm only doing what any red-blooded American would do," he said in a shaky voice, still uncomfortable speaking in public, but trying his best to rally the crowd. "We're gonna do our part, and we'll win, 'cause we're on God's side."

The crowd roared with approval, and by the time Joe's alarm clock rang the following morning, Americans across the country were echoing his words: "We'll win because we are on God's side." Newspapers ran the phrase in their headlines. Soon, poets would write verses based on it. Musicians would compose songs around it.

As fast as it could print them, the military distributed recruitment posters showing Joe in his Army uniform, holding a rifle with a bayonet attached. The poster read: PVT. JOE LOUIS SAYS, "WE'RE GOING TO DO OUR PART . . . AND WE'LL WIN BECAUSE WE'RE ON GOD'S SIDE."

As it happened, Joe was never asked to fire the rifle he'd held in the recruitment poster. His job was to build morale by visiting with soldiers and performing boxing exhibitions, which he did with great enthusiasm. In all, he would stage ninety-six fights for American troops stationed in the United States and abroad. When someone asked him how it felt to be fighting for nothing, he

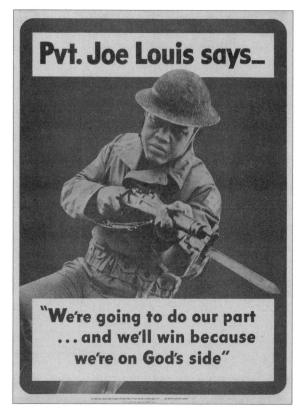

Joe appears on an American recruitment poster.

said, "I ain't fighting for nothing, I'm fighting for my Country."

Despite all that Joe did for his country—including walking away from millions of dollars in fight purses for a soldier's pay of $21 a month—he was still a black man, and still subject to the country's systemic racism.

Like much of America, the U.S. military was rigidly segregated by race. Even on army bases as far north as

New York and New Jersey, Joe was relegated to the "colored" barracks.

"Here are all these 'niggers' ready and willing to go out and try to kill Hitler, and maybe get themselves killed," he said. "But they can't sleep in the same barracks with the white guys, or go to the same movies, or hardly get in officer's training."

Joe fought back by refusing to perform in theatrical productions in segregated camps and boycotting boxing exhibitions at segregated bases.

In 1942, while in Fort Riley, Kansas, to complete his basic training, he met a soldier named Jackie Robinson—the same Jackie Robinson who'd go on to integrate major league baseball. Robinson had been drafted into the army and assigned to an all-black cavalry unit at Fort Riley. Fresh out of UCLA, the young Robinson was a standout athlete, and when he was told he wouldn't be allowed to play on the all-white baseball team, he responded by refusing to play on its football team as well. Joe, holding more sway than other black soldiers, went to the commanding general and spoke up for Robinson. Shortly thereafter, orders arrived from Washington: Robinson, and any other black soldiers, could play on whatever team they liked.

On another occasion, Joe and future welterweight champion Sugar Ray Robinson were at a bus depot at Camp Sibert, Alabama, waiting to be transported to

Private Joe Louis reports for duty.

nearby Birmingham to stage a boxing exhibition. When Joe went inside to use the station's only pay phone, which was located in the "whites only" section, a military policeman ordered the two men to move to the "colored" area of the facility.

"I'm a soldier like any other American soldier," Joe told the MP. "I don't want to be pushed to the back because I'm a Negro."

The two boxers were arrested and put in the camp stockade, but when Joe threatened to call Washington, the post commander released them. The incident made headlines, most prominently in the black press, and the Army responded by integrating its bus stations.

Meanwhile, the war was slogging on with no end in sight. The Nazi agenda—exterminating all Jews living in its territory—was well underway. American forces landed in Great Britain to join the fight against Hitler. German U-boats launched an offensive along the East Coast of the United States.

For Joe, hardship wasn't limited to the military. It hit his personal life, too. While at his first post, at Camp Upton on Long Island, he received word that Chappie Blackburn had died of a heart attack. Joe immediately received a leave of absence and went to his apartment in New York. There, he lay across his bed and wept. He hadn't experienced this kind of emotional pain since he'd lost his stepfather, Pat Brooks. Days later, he went to Chicago for the funeral and honored Chappie by serving as one of his pallbearers.

"I loved that Chappie," Joe said. "When the dirt went down on that coffin, I knew my life would never be the same again."

He had no idea how right he was.

Crawling Through Rubble

In April 1945, Max was back home on his estate with Anny, nursing his injuries. He figured he was safely removed from the battlefields, until Soviet forces started approaching from the east. At the rate they were going, they would reach Max's farm in an hour or two. Max had no idea what would happen when they got there, and didn't wait to find out.

He and Anny packed their bags and fled. On the road, they charted the quickest path to safety. Anny would head north. Max would venture to their apartment in Berlin, gather the rest of their possessions, and join her in Rostock.

The plan went smoothly until Max reached Berlin. The city had already been bombed to its knees. Dark plumes of smoke spiraled from the wreckage of crumbling buildings, filling the red, glowing sky with black soot. He met up with some old friends and walked the desolate streets, climbing around bomb craters and mounds of debris, breathing in the dust, dirt, and ashes that filled the air.

In Max's words, "the city had become a waiting room for the final catastrophe."

The wait wasn't long. The Soviet army had advanced to within thirty-five miles of the capital. More Soviet forces lay to the north and south, preparing to encircle the city. Soon, tanks would begin steamrolling down the boulevards. Max knew it was time to get out. At three o'clock in the morning, he got back in his car and headed north, watching the city slowly disappear in his rearview mirror.

As Germany crumbled, its führer, Adolf Hitler, hid in an underground bunker near the Reich Chancellery,

The Soviet army occupies bombed-out Berlin at the end of the war.

which was also under siege. Rather than die at the hands of his enemies, he downed a cyanide pill, but didn't bother waiting for the poison to kill him. He grabbed his gun, put it to his head, and fired.

Days later, Germany surrendered.

Benito Mussolini, also knowing he'd be punished for war crimes, tried to escape Italy, but he was captured by partisans and executed.

In two separate attacks in early August, the United States dropped atom bombs on Hiroshima and Nagasaki, annihilating both Japanese cities and killing and maiming more than two hundred thousand citizens. Within days, Emperor Hirohito announced Japan's surrender.

World War II was finally over. In six years, the war had taken the lives of sixty million people and crippled countless others. Max, despite having earned a million dollars in the ring, was all but wiped out. He couldn't access his money because the Soviets had closed the banks in Berlin, and the Allies had rendered German reichsmarks all but worthless.

The country Max loved was gone forever.

He hoped to go back to the United States, but American newspapers made it clear that he wasn't welcome. The influential sportswriter John Lardner, who had served as a war correspondent, wrote, "I hope there is no doubt about the position of Herr Schmeling. . . . If there is, any number of people in the neighborhood of the fight beat, including myself, will cheerfully testify that there is no more cold, pronounced, unpleasant, and natural a Nazi in all the ranks of the party and its sympathizers."

Max fought back, saying he'd never officially joined the Nazi Party. But it didn't matter. American boxing promoters were no longer interested. He tried to rejoin the fight game in Germany, but his once-famous right hand had lost its luster. And so, in 1947, he walked away from the sport for good.

Hanging Up the Gloves

In 1945, Joe's infidelities caught up with him. He and Marva, now the parents of two-year-old Jacqueline, ended their marriage, leaving Joe to fend for himself. Chappie was gone, and both of Joe's managers, John Roxborough and Julian Black, were out of the picture. Roxborough had been convicted of running a numbers racket and was serving thirty months in prison. Black had also had a run-in with the law—he'd been indicted on tax evasion in a case that was dismissed—but his funds had run dry and he and Joe parted ways. Joe and Marva would remarry and have another child, Joe Louis Barrow Jr., but the marriage would crumble a second time, again due to Joe's betrayals.

"Even giving her everything I thought she wanted, I wasn't really giving enough," Joe said by way of explanation. "I had no intention of being faithful—too many pretty girls out there."

Joe returned to the ring in 1946. Over the previous four years, he had fought only once—a glorified four-round exhibition—and needed to pay the bills. He defended his title against Billy Conn, a beefed-up light heavyweight who'd given him trouble five years earlier. He put Conn away in eight rounds, but his age was beginning to show; he was slower and nowhere near as sharp as he'd been in his prime.

So, after a few more fights, including two against Jersey Joe Walcott, Joe hung up his gloves. In 1949, he walked away from the sport he loved, and he did so as a winner. He'd held the title for eleven years and nine months, making twenty-five successful defenses. No heavyweight champion had ever reigned for so long or defended his title as many times. His official record was 58-1, his only loss coming in his first fight against Max Schmeling. As far as America was concerned, Joe Louis was the greatest heavyweight in history.

CHAPTER 10

Joe at the Bottom

The country's beloved Brown Bomber wasn't able to bask in the glory of his achievements. The fight game had brought him more riches than he'd ever imagined—he'd earned more than $4 million in the ring—yet he still found himself in a financial hole. Some of his wealth had gone to noble causes, such as a house for his brothers and sisters, and tuition for college and graduate school for his sister Vunies, but he'd blown the rest of it on hangers-on, adoring women, and shady money managers. He'd also bought into one losing investment after another: an apartment building in Chicago, a horse farm in Michigan, a nightclub in Chicago, and a fried chicken joint in Detroit.

Sportswriter Wendell Smith recalled how the champ had wined and dined his entourage: "In a night club, he never drank anything stronger than a coke, never smoked a cigarette or a cigar. . . . Yet the bill could be as high as $1,000 and it wasn't padded. . . . Joe would grab the check, argue if someone else wanted to pick it up."

In 1950, thirty-six years old and broke, Joe returned to the ring and won eight of his next nine fights. The following October, he took on a promising heavyweight named Rocky Marciano. For those who wanted to preserve their memories of Joe as an unbeatable champion—and as the American icon who'd conquered Nazism—the fight was painful to watch. Marciano, who was nine years younger than Joe and undefeated in thirty-seven fights, spent the first seven rounds pounding Joe and, in the eighth, sent him tumbling backward through the ropes. A pitiful figure, Joe lay on his back, his right foot hanging limply on the lowest rung, his head dangling off the edge of the ring apron.

In his dressing room after the fight, Joe told the roomful of reporters, "I saw the right hand coming, but I couldn't do anything about it. I was awfully tired. I'm too old, I guess."

Joe's incredible ride in the ring was finally over. But a new fight, one with the U.S. government, was just beginning.

At the time, the federal tax rate for high-income earners was ninety percent, and the Internal Revenue Service (IRS) hit Joe with a bill for $600,000. He had no way of raising that kind of money, and as he searched for work, his debt continued to mount. In six years,

At thirty-seven, Joe is finished.

interest and penalties drove the tab up to $1.25 million. To pay it off, Joe would have had to earn a million dollars a year for the rest of his life, which was impossible. It's true that he was still tied to several businesses—the Joe Louis Milk Company in Chicago, the Louis & Rowe public relations firm in New York, the Joe Louis Food Franchise

Corporation—but his income from those enterprises amounted to very little. The debt was so staggering, and the law so convoluted, that Joe could barely figure out what he owed, or to whom he owed it.

"One tax guy went over my finances," he said. "[He] found out I had been borrowing money from my own companies and hadn't paid taxes on the money I borrowed. I don't know, he might as well have been talking Greek to me. What I did know was I had no money."

In an effort to scratch together a living he turned to show business, hoping his name still carried some weight

Trying to make ends meet, Joe takes to the wrestling ring.

at the box office. He took the stage in Las Vegas, skipping a glow-in-the-dark rope alongside showgirls, and shadow-boxing with entertainer Pearl Bailey. He performed a comedy routine at the Apollo Theater in Harlem, and toured the South with rhythm-and-blues singer Ruth Brown. His biggest payday likely came from the game show *High Finance*, on which he and his second wife, Rose Morgan, won more than $50,000. (Joe's half went directly to the IRS.) He even turned to pro wrestling and "fought" the likes of Bozo Brown for a couple of hundred bucks per appearance. The money paid a few bills, but didn't make a dent in his outsized debt.

Max at the Top

In 1954, while visiting the United States, Max got in touch with Jim Farley, an old friend from the New York State Athletic Commission. Farley was now running Coca-Cola's exporting business and was looking for a way into the European market. Max seemed like a good fit. Although convicted by the American public, he had been cleared of any collusion with the Nazis by a British military court. And, so, Farley made Max the offer of a lifetime: a Coca-Cola franchise in northern Germany, with exclusive manufacturing, bottling, and distribution rights. Max became a goodwill ambassador for the soda company, appearing on television, at sporting events, and in public venues, always drinking from a bottle of

Max shilling for Coca-Cola.

Coke. His new company was soon pumping money as easily as it did soda.

It had been a long, bumpy ride, but Max now had a thriving business in Hamburg, the same city where he'd fallen in love with boxing and spent nights watching the great Jack Dempsey at the local movie theater. And perhaps even more ironic, after Max was vilified as a Nazi, he made his fortune with Coca-Cola, a quintessentially American company.

This Is Your Life

In 1960, at the age of forty-six, Joe was the guest of honor on *This Is Your Life*, a national television program in which the host, Ralph Edwards, paid tribute to celebrities by parading out people from their past. Joe greeted the guests while standing on the stage in a bow tie and tuxedo, his face rounder and his stomach softer than they'd been in his younger years. James Braddock came out to shake hands with the champ, as did John Roxborough and Julian Black. But the biggest surprise was yet to come. The show's producers had found Max Schmeling on vacation in Switzerland and flown him to New York to meet with his onetime adversary.

When Schmeling bounded out from behind the curtain, slim and robust in a gray tailored suit, the audience gave him a hearty ovation—and Joe greeted him with a broad, welcoming smile. Joe was obviously happy, and shocked, to see the man the world had repeatedly told him was his archenemy. If any bad blood still lingered between America and Germany, it obviously didn't sway either fighter. The two clasped hands—the same hands that had once targeted each other's temples.

"Great to see you, Max," Joe said. "You haven't put on any weight."

"Nice to see you, too," Schmeling said, embracing Joe. "You are looking great."

Ralph Edwards interviewed Schmeling, leading him through a recollection of how he'd once floored Joe with his overhand right. Then, of course, they spoke of Joe's revenge in the big fight, the one that foreshadowed World War II. Schmeling had nothing but praise for Joe, in and out of the ring.

"He's the biggest sportsman and the finest sportsman I ever met," he said. "Joe, all good luck to you and to your family."

"Thank you," Joe said, still smiling.

It was a pleasant affair. But those in the know couldn't ignore the paradox. Here was Joe Louis, the symbol of American democracy, destitute, alongside Max Schmeling, the German fighter who'd come to represent the Nazi regime, rich off profits from an American company.

It didn't seem to bother Joe.

EPILOGUE

"Let's Hear It for the Champ"

In November 1978, two thousand people crammed into the gilded ballroom of Las Vegas's Caesars Palace for "A Night with the Champ." The lavish party, which was thrown by world-famous singer Frank Sinatra in Joe's honor, attracted celebrities from all spheres of society. Again Max Schmeling showed up to support his former rival. The evening was a thank-you to Joe for all he had done for his country.

But the glitz and glamour were a façade.

Joe's life had skidded into a hole of despair from which he had no means of climbing out. He'd undergone heart surgery and suffered a stroke a year earlier, and had entered the ballroom in a wheelchair pushed by Sinatra. His tax issues had finally been settled; his third wife, attorney Martha Jefferson, had made a deal with the government. The good news was that Joe would only have to pay taxes on his future income. But his earning potential had evaporated; he was now dependent almost exclusively on the generosity of friends. What's more, Joe had been fighting a cocaine addiction for several years, and the drug was battering him far worse than any boxer ever had.

"I guess I been around this stuff a long time with all these show people who took it," he said. "I started when I was feeling bad, but I never was strung out on it. Just makes me feel relaxed."

Perhaps the result of the drugs, or of having taken too many punches to the head, Joe was also suffering from paranoid delusions. He'd become unhinged, convinced that the government was tapping his phones, recording his conversations, and threatening his life. He'd even taped up the air vents in his bedroom, for fear that the Mafia would kill him with poisonous gas. His mental state had deteriorated so badly that Martha and his son Joseph Barrow Jr. brought him to a psychiatric hospital. There, doctors put him on a regimen of medications that tempered his delusions—but couldn't turn back the clock.

In short, the world had passed Joe by. The young generation saw him as yesterday's news, an out-of-touch champion who'd never stood up to the establishment, a champion who may have represented his race, but never took a public stand for it. It was the 1960s, a time of unparalleled social upheaval, and an era that introduced a new breed of athlete. As millions of people were demonstrating against the Vietnam War and marching for civil rights, heavyweight champion Muhammad Ali spoke out against white authority and refused military induction on the grounds of his Muslim faith. Ali was stripped of his title for three-and-a-half years, and by willingly taking that punishment, he had shown the kind of courage that young people rallied around. Here was a black man who'd confronted the government, who'd fought for his rights, who'd stood up for his beliefs. In their eyes, Joe had done none of those things.

Three years after Sinatra's party, Joe was back at Caesars. On April 11, 1981, he was wheeled to the edge of the ring to watch Larry Holmes defend his heavyweight title against Canadian champion Trevor Berbick. It turned out to be Joe's last public appearance. The following morning, he had a heart attack at home and died a few hours later in Desert Springs Hospital. He was sixty-six.

Three thousand mourners came to Las Vegas for Joe's funeral. The Reverend Jesse Louis Jackson, who was named after Joe, eulogized the former champion.

"God sent Joe from the black race to represent the human race," Jackson told the massive gathering. "He was the answer to the sincere prayers of the disinherited and dispossessed. Let's give Joe a big handclap. This is a celebration. Let's hear it for the champ. Let's hear it for the champ!"

The crowd rose to its feet and gave a standing ovation

for the imperfect man who had once carried the honor of his race and country on his back.

In death, Joe was a hero again.

Even the American government gave him a long over-due acknowledgement. Despite Joe's never having seen active duty, President Ronald Reagan waived the eligibility rules for Arlington National Cemetery and authorized a burial with full military honors. Joe's body was flown to Virginia where he was laid to rest alongside American soldiers, politicians, and presidents.

At Joe's burial, boxing champions Muhammad Ali, Joe Frazier, Sugar Ray Robinson, Sugar Ray Leonard, Jersey Joe Walcott, and Billy Conn surrounded his casket. So did hundreds of young mourners, both black and white. They'd come to honor the heavyweight champion who'd represented their parents' generation, the black man who'd inspired millions of oppressed people to pray in front of their radios, the one-time factory worker who'd beaten the Nazis.

Forever Linked

Max continued to live a prosperous life long after his old nemesis, Joe Louis, passed away. He kept his body strong by riding his bike and hunting on his land, and he kept his reputation polished by making public appearances and writing three autobiographies. In 1987, his wife, Anny died, and Max remained in their house in

Hollenstedt, near Hamburg, alone, surrounded by nature, still prosperous.

On February 2, 2005, Max's body finally quit, and at the age of ninety-nine, he died of natural causes. Until his dying day, he was asked about his ties to Hitler, and he continued to disavow any allegiance to the Nazi Party.

"I would have stayed [in America]," he once said, explaining why he'd chosen to remain in Nazi Germany during the war. "But my mother and wife lived in Germany. I was worried the Nazis would do something if I didn't return."

Max has since been memorialized in Germany. A bust of the one-time champion stands in Hollenstedt, and Germans flock to the Max Schmeling Hall in Berlin. In 2005, on what would have been his hundredth birthday, the German government issued a postage stamp with his likeness.

Across the Atlantic, Joe Louis was featured on a U.S. stamp in 1993. In downtown Detroit, the city where Joe launched his boxing career, a twenty-four-foot-long bronze sculpture of his clenched right fist is on display. In Pompton Lakes, New Jersey, the site of his old training camp, Americans stroll Joe Louis Memorial Park. In LaFayette, Alabama, an eight-foot-high statue of the city's hometown hero guards the county courthouse.

And so, the two fighters will continue to flex their muscles and raise their fists long into the future. Times will change, young generations will mature, and new governments will come into power. And through it all, Joe Louis and Max Schmeling will endure, forever linked, as the pair of champions who represented their countries in the greatest war ever fought in the ring.

Joe and Max reunite in 1966.

ACKNOWLEDGMENTS

This book owes its origin to our editors, Simon Boughton and Katherine Jacobs. Simon sat down for coffee with our agent, Jennifer Weltz, and shared his idea: to tell the story of Joe Louis and Max Schmeling, and the historical events that shaped their lives. Katherine took the baton and helped bring the story to life. Thank you, Simon, Katherine, and Jennifer, for trusting us with such weighty material—and for your much-needed help along the way.

When re-creating scenes, both in and out of the ring, we set out to be true to history. And so we acknowledge the legions of journalists who covered these stories as they happened. They provided us with the richest material, keeping our journey interesting and rewarding.

Lastly, we thank Joe Louis and Max Schmeling. This is their story.

SOURCE NOTES

Prologue

The second Louis-Schmeling fight has been well documented. We've pulled from a variety of newspapers published at the time as well as two books: David Margolick's *Beyond the Glory*, and Lewis A. Erenberg's *Greatest Fight of Our Generation*.

Chapter 1

The information about America during the Depression has been covered extensively. We gathered this information, as well as Joe's personal experiences, from newspaper accounts of the day, especially those in the *Detroit Free Press*. We used several biographies, most notably Robert Lipsyte's *Joe Louis: A Champ for All America*, Richard Bak's *Joe Louis: The Great Black Hope*, and Chris Mead's *Joe Louis: Black Champion in White America*.

The stories of Joe's adolescence, including his conversations with Thurston McKinney and his experiences at the Brewster recreation center, came from "My Story—Joe Louis," which appeared in *Life* magazine, November 8 and 15, 1948. We also relied on John U. Bacon's article in the *Detroit News and Free Press*, June 22, 1997.

All of Joe's quotes, including his conversations with

Pat Brooks and Holman Williams, as well as the stories about John Roxborough, Julian Black, and Jack "Chappie" Blackburn, were taken from the above sources, along with his autobiographies, *My Life Story* in 1947 and *Joe Louis: My Life* in 1978.

The Jack "Chappie" Blackburn quote about Joe having to knock out his opponents is compiled from two different sources: Joe Louis's *My Life Story*, and Chris Mead's *Joe Louis: Black Champion in White America.*

The discussion of the Jim Crow South in early twentieth-century America was based on W. E. B. DuBois's *Souls of Black Folk* and PBS's 2002 series *The Rise and Fall of Jim Crow.*

The story of Jack Johnson was taken from many sources, primarily Thomas Hietala's *Fight of the Century* and Randy Roberts's *Papa Jack*. We also relied on reports from July 5, 1910, published by the *Salt Lake Tribune* and the *Greenville News* of South Carolina, as well as articles written by Jack Johnson that appeared in the *Pittsburgh Courier* on April 20 and April 27, 1929.

The columnist who predicted Joe would be a serious contender was George A. Barton of the *Minneapolis Tribune* in his Sportographs column, December 6, 1934. Chester Washington of the *Pittsburgh Courier* likened Joe to a frozen cucumber in his Sez Ches column, December 22, 1934.

Chapter 2

We found the story of Joe refusing to eat watermelon in Barney Nagler's "The Brown Bomber" run by *Sport* magazine in March 1960.

Chester Washington commented about Joe's sparring sessions in his Sez Ches column in the *Pittsburgh Courier*, June 8, 1935. Seal Harris's words appeared in George Barton's article, "Joe Louis Can Have Baer, Schmeling Fights, If He Wins," in the *Minneapolis Tribune*, June 22, 1935. We changed the quote from "Ah'm glad Ah'm gettin' outta here alive" to "I'm glad I'm getting out of here alive" to remove the racist overtone cast by the white newspaper.

The stories of Joe's arrival at Penn Station were taken from his autobiography *My Life Story*, as were his quotes about the Carnera fight.

The scene in which Joe meets FDR at the White House was taken from the *Baltimore Afro-American* of September 7, 1935. ("President Felt Joe Louis's Muscle; Told Him He's a Fine-looking Young Man.")

Countless newspapers covered Joe's wedding to Marva. We relied on "I've a Date with a Fellow Named Max Baer, Joe Louis' Parting Words to His Wife," in the *Philadelphia Inquirer*, and "Louis Marries Before Fight" in the *Pittsburgh Post-Gazette*, both September 25, 1935.

Joe's quote about Baer looking as trim as a greyhound

and tanned as a hickory nut is from his autobiography, *My Life Story.*

We re-created Joe's fight with Max Baer by reading historical accounts and viewing archival footage. The part about Baer's manager, Ancil Hoffman, promoting Baer's heritage is from Mike Silver's *Stars in the Ring.* The part about Jack Dempsey imploring Baer to stand up and fight is from *The Rochester Democrat and Chronicle,* September 25, 1935.

The story of Joe at Detroit's Calvary Baptist Church is from the *Philadelphia Tribune* of October 3, 1935. ("Detroit Turns Out To Greet Brown Bomber: 7,500 Crowd Church Many Others Watch From Streets.")

Chapter 3

We built the scenes of Max's younger years using several sources, including *Max Schmeling: An Autobiography* and two series of newspaper articles: One was autobiographical and appeared in the *Montana Standard* (Butte) over two weeks in February 1929; we used the February 12 and 13 installments in particular. The other was Werner Laufer's "The Life Story of Max Schmeling," which was syndicated in papers across the country in six parts by the Newspaper Enterprise Association in June 1930.

Information on Jack Dempsey was largely taken from Randy Roberts's *Jack Dempsey: The Manassa Mauler.*

Max's quote about America ("Before me rose

America . . .") is from his article in the *Montana Standard* (Butte), February 19, 1929.

Max's ring career and those of his opponents were sourced at the archive on BoxRec.com. His personal recollections were taken from his autobiography and Patrick Myler's *Ring of Hate*.

Dr. Wilfred Fralick's quote about Max's fitness was taken from "Surgeon Calls Turn on Maxie" in the *Wilkes-Barre (PA) Record*, May 20, 1930.

Tex Rickard's quote is from David Pfeifer's book, *Max Schmeling*.

We read about the sportswriter suggesting Max's left hand was only useful for holding a fork in David Margolick's *Beyond Glory*.

James J. Corbett's opinion of Max was taken from his article in the *St. Louis Star* on June 26, 1929, "Schmeling Is No 'Second Dempsey,' Corbett Declares."

Max's quote about being a hero after the Risko fight is from his article in the *Montana Standard* (Butte), February 23, 1929.

All ring-related stories were compiled from historical newspaper accounts.

Chapter 4

When re-creating the brouhaha surrounding Jack Sharkey's disqualification, we relied heavily on Perry Lewis's coverage in the *Philadelphia Inquirer*, June 13 and 14, 1930.

Joe Jacobs's quote "You wuz fouled" is from the Western Newspaper Union wire service. We found it in the *Lehi Free Press* of May 16, 1940.

Hitler's treatment of Jews and "undesirables" has been documented in many historical texts. We relied on many, especially Milton Mayer's *They Thought They Were Free.*

Details of the second Schmeling-Sharkey fight were found in a number of sources, particularly Westbrook Pegler's coverage in the *Chicago Daily Tribune,* June 22 and 23, 1932. We also relied on articles by Damon Runyon, Jack Sharkey, and Havey J. Boyle in the *Pittsburgh Post-Gazette* on June 22, 1932, and the piece by Perry Lewis in the *Philadelphia Inquirer,* also on June 22, 1932.

W. O. McGeehan's quote about foreign fighters is from the Associated Press article "Metropolitan Scribes Kick On Decision." We found it in the *Press and Sun-Bulletin* (Binghamton, NY), June 22, 1938.

Mayor Jimmy Walker's quote was picked up by the wire services. We took it from Pegler's article, June 22, 1932.

Max's viewpoints and quotes, including the stories of Joe Jacobs coming to Germany, being refused a room at the Hotel Bristol, and giving the Nazi salute, are from *Max Schmeling: An Autobiography,* as is Max's conversation with Hitler at the Reich Chancellery. The ruckus surrounding Jacobs's salute can also be found in "Jacobs

Kindles Maxie Boycott" by Jack Miley in the New York *Daily News*, March 22, 1935. The incident at the Hotel Bristol is also in Patrick Myler's *Ring of Hate*.

We found Max's meeting with Avery Brundage in Max's autobiography and Lewis A. Erenberg's *Greatest Fight of Our Generation*.

The details surrounding Max's meeting with the New York State Athletic Commission (along with Max's conversation with Phelan) can be found in the AP story picked up by the *Montgomery Advertiser*, December 11, 1935.

The conversation between Max and reporters ("I saw something") is from *Max Schmeling: An Autobiography*.

We re-created the fights in this chapter by reading historical accounts and watching films.

Chapter 5

Joe's quote about buying custom suits is from "Part 2 of Joe Louis' Story," as told to Meyer Berger and Barney Nagler, in *Life*, November 15, 1948.

Joe's love of drugstores was mentioned in sports editor William B. Loftus's Evening Chatter column in the *Evening News* of Wilkes-Barre, Pennsylvania, June 16, 1936. We changed the quote ("Ah got mah mother all fixed up" to "I got my mother all fixed up") to remove the racist overtone cast by the white newspaper.

The stories of Joe's training camp in Lakewood, New Jersey, including those of his sparring partners, were carried on the wire services of the day. We relied on Associated Press reporter Eddie Brietz, June 10, 1936, and United Press sportswriters George Kirksey, May 25, 1936, and Henry McLemore, May 27, 1936. We also turned to Robert A. Pelham's "Brown Bomber Has 'Happy Family' At Camp" in the *Atlanta Daily World,* June 4, 1936.

Joe's quote about his extramarital affairs is from his 1978 autobiography, *Joe Louis: My Life.*

The stories from Max's training camp in Napanoch, New York, are also from the wire services. We took Max's quotes from an Associated Press story on June 9, 1936.

Jimmy Cannon's quote about hunger being a fighter's best friend is from David Margolick's *Beyond Glory.*

The fight scenes were taken from various archival materials. Joe's thoughts inside the ring and his reaction afterward are from his 1947 autobiography, *My Life Story.* We transcribed Clem McCarthy's call of the first Louis-Schmeling bout from a film of the fight as aired on *Ringside* (ESPN Classic, 2007).

The scene of Joe in his locker room after the fight was taken from his 1947 autobiography. Jack "Chappie" Blackburn's quote was reported by George Kirksey of the United Press on June 20, 1936. We found it in the *Kane (PA) Republican* of the same date ("Schmeling's Feat Stuns Sports

World"). Joe's quote about his stepfather comes from the second installment of his story in *Life* magazine, November 15, 1948.

We took the Langston Hughes quote about Harlem's reaction to Joe's loss from the *Collected Works of Langston Hughes*.

The part about the U.S. Congress coming to a standstill after the first Louis-Schmeling fight is from the United Press. We found it in the *Atlanta Constitution*, June 20, 1936.

William McG. Keefe's quote about boxing's reign of terror is from Marcy S. Sacks's *Joe Louis: Sports and Race in Twentieth-Century America*.

Chapter 6

The story of Max's return to Germany after defeating Louis can be found in Max's autobiography. It can also be found in his obituary in the *Los Angeles Times*, February 5, 2005, "Max Schmeling, 99; Boxer Became, for a Time, Symbol of Nazi Germany After Defeating Louis," by Earl Gustkey. The scene of his meeting with Hitler at the Reich Chancellery, including what was said there, was compiled from his autobiography and from Albion Ross's coverage in the *New York Times*, June 27, 1936. The quotes from the Nazi newspapers were found in the *New York Times*, June 28, 1936, and England's *Manchester Guardian*, June 26, 1936.

Hitler's scrubbing Berlin of Nazi propaganda before the 1936 Olympics is covered in many publications. We relied heavily on David Clay Large's *Nazi Games* and Albion Ross's account of the preparations in the *New York Times*, December 15, 1935.

Max's quote about Jesse Owens flying like the Hindenburg is from the *Pittsburgh Courier*, "Owens Runs like the Hindenburg Flies—Schmeling," August 15, 1936. We found it in Jeremy Schaap's *Triumph: The Untold Story of Jesse Owens and Hitler's Olympics*.

The details of the backroom deal are explained in Jeremy Schaap's *Cinderella Man*.

We re-created the Braddock-Louis fight from news accounts of the day, films of the fight, and Jeremy Schaap's *Cinderella Man*.

James Braddock's quotes were found in the *Sports Illustrated* article "Joe Louis' Biggest Fights," May 13, 2014.

Chappie's dynamite quote was reported in the *New York Evening Journal*, June 23, 1937. We found it in David Margolick's *Beyond Glory*. We changed "shoa" to "sure" to remove the racist overtone cast by the white newspaper.

Joe's thoughts during the Braddock fight are taken from his 1947 autobiography. His quote about not being champ until he beats Schmeling is from John U. Bacon's "First title for Louis began incredible streak as champ" in the *Detroit Free Press*, June 22, 1997.

Chapter 7

Max's cut for the rematch and his comments were reported by Alan Gould of the Associated Press, September 5, 1937. The *Pittsburgh Courier*'s James Edmund Boyack reported Max's trash talk. We found Max's quote about crossing the Atlantic eight times in an article written by Harry Grayson of the Newspaper Enterprise Association, June 13, 1938.

The story of Hitler joining forces with Mussolini and Hirohito has been explored by many historians. We used William L. Shirer's *Rise and Fall of the Third Reich*.

The events surrounding Max's arrival in New York were taken from *Max Schmeling: An Autobiography*.

To re-create Joe's training camp, we relied on Joseph Monninger's *Two Ton: One Night, One Fight*. Joe's words about Max representing everything Americans disliked are from his 1978 autobiography. Joe's comment that he had learned to fight since the last Schmeling bout was reported by the Associated Press, June 22, 1938.

Harry Thomas's "snus" comment was reported by Steve Snider of the United Press, April 2, 1938. The "stretched my neck" comment was carried by the Associated Press, April 3, 1938.

Joe wrote of his retort to Jimmy Cannon in his 1978 autobiography.

Jersey Joe Walcott talked about Camden on the night

of the fight with Ira Berkow of the *New York Times* in "Nation Remembers Deeds of Joe Louis," August 28, 1982.

President Jimmy Carter reminisced about listening to the fight in HBO's 2008 documentary *Joe Louis: America's Hero Betrayed.*

The descriptions of Max and Joe in their dressing rooms before the fight came from the two fighters' autobiographies.

Mike Jacobs's pep talk is from Jack Newfield's article, "Joe Louis Strikes a Blow for Democracy," in the *New York Post*, October 3, 1999. We changed the phrasing to avoid using profanity.

The scenes of Joe and Max approaching the ring are taken from films of the fight and David Margolick's *Beyond Glory.*

Chapter 8

The prefight scene in the ring was taken from films of the fight. The same is true for Harry Balogh's introductions, and the match itself. The boxers' thoughts and reactions are from their autobiographies.

We picked up Joe's quotes—"felt like a racehorse" and "whole career depended on the fight"—from his 1978 autobiography.

The Clem McCarthy radio call was taken from a recording posted by National Public Radio on its website.

The Arno Helmis call was taken from "Tragedy on the Air Waves!" in the *Pittsburgh Press* of July 31, 1938.

To re-create the crowd reaction within Yankee Stadium, we relied on several newspaper accounts of the day.

The *New York Journal and American* reported Max's champion comment, June 23, 1938. We found it in David Margolick's *Beyond Glory*. We picked up "He has beat me" from an Associated Press story, "'Ah'm Sho' Nuff Champeen Now,'" June 23, 1938.

The scene of Mayor La Guardia in Joe's dressing room is described in Irwin Silber's *Press Box Red: The Story of Lester Rodney*.

The victory celebration in Harlem has been written about extensively. Richard Wright described it in "High Tide in Harlem: Joe Louis as a Symbol of Freedom," which ran in *New Masses*, July 5, 1938. We picked up the part about the shoeshine boys in Barney Nagler's "The Brown Bomber" in *Sport* magazine, March 1960. Lewis Valentine's quote is from "Harlem Celebrants Toss Varied Missiles," *New York Times*, June 23, 1938.

The celebration in Chicago's South Side is from the *Pittsburgh Courier* of July 2, 1938.

The celebratory scene in Philadelphia, Pennsylvania, is from Kent Jackson's article in the *Philadelphia Tribune*, June 23, 1938.

The celebratory scene in Camden, New Jersey, and Jersey Joe Walcott's quote are from Ira Berkow's "Nation

Remembers Deeds of Joe Louis" in the *New York Times*, August 28, 1982.

The celebratory scene in Detroit is from "Paradise Valley Dances for Joy as Its Joe Wins," *Detroit Free Press*, June 23, 1938, and John Bacon's retrospective in the paper, June 22, 1997.

Lillie Barrow's address sometimes appears as McDougall Street and other times as McDougall Avenue. We took 2100 McDougall Avenue from the *Detroit Free Press*, "News of Joe Louis' Victory Launches Wild Celebration," August 8, 1935.

The celebratory scene at Jimmy Carter's home in Georgia is from the HBO documentary *Joe Louis: America's Hero Betrayed*.

The comment about the white southern press grudgingly praising Joe is from Jeffrey T. Sammons's article, "Boxing as a Reflection of Society: The Southern Reaction to Joe Louis." (*The Journal of Popular Culture*, Spring 1983.)

The scene of Joe and Marva celebrating at the Harlem home of Christopher Savage is from the International News Service, "Louis Feasts on Ice Cream after Battle," published in the *Evening News* of Wilkes-Barre, Pennsylvania, June 23, 1938.

We discovered Bill Gaither's "Champ Joe Louis" and the existence of nearly fifty other songs in Bill Margolick's "Only One Athlete Has Ever Inspired This Many Songs," in the *New York Times*, February 25, 2001.

"Champ Joe Louis" can be heard on YouTube, youtube.com /watch?v=_1HV5lGUbvE.

Jimmy Cannon's quote has been repeated in countless journals and articles. We found it in his obituary by Dave Anderson in the *New York Times*, December 6, 1973.

Chapter 9

We found the story of Max leaving the Polyclinic Hospital and returning home to Germany in Lew Freedman's *Joe Louis: The Life of a Heavyweight*. There are conflicting reports as to the number of broken vertebrae. We took our diagnosis from David Margolick's obituary of Max in the *New York Times*, February 5, 2005.

Max's presence at the Nuremberg rally is from *Max Schmeling: An Autobiography*. His comments on his status after losing to Louis are from Bill Cunningham's article, which ran in the *Pittsburgh Post-Gazette*, July 17, 1945.

The story of Max saving Henri and Werner Lewin has been told in many venues. We relied heavily on Henri's account. He talked about the experience nearly fifty years later with Earl Gustkey of the *Los Angeles Times* ("When Schmeling Risked It All," December 23, 1989).

Max's move to the countryside and his farmhand's observation on the invasion of Poland are from Max's autobiography.

Max's episode in the Third Paratroop Regiment is a popular story. We found details in war correspondent Hal Boyle's "Schmeling Death and Burial Would Satisfy Captain," which appeared in the *Muncie (IN) Evening Press*, August 1, 1944; Bill Cunningham's postwar interview with the fighter, which appeared in the *Pittsburgh Post-Gazette*, July 17 and 18, 1945; and Max's interview with Bill McCormick of the Newspaper Enterprise Association, which ran in newspapers on January 14, 1961.

We read about Joe's donation to the Navy Relief Fund in Dave Anderson's column in the *New York Times*, April 20, 1981.

Joe's quote about being glad to defend America is from Thomas R. Hietala's *Fight of the Century*.

We re-created the rally at Madison Square Garden, including Joe's quote about being on God's side, using a number of sources, most notably Melancholy Jones's "Sport Slants" column in the *Atlanta Daily World* of March 27, 1942.

Joe's "I ain't fighting for nothing" quote is from the Iffy the Dopester column in the *Detroit Free Press*, January 13, 1942; Joe's "Here are all these 'niggers'" quote comes from his 1978 autobiography. We found it in Richard Bak's *Joe Louis: The Great Black Hope*.

We found Joe's monthly pay of $21 in Lew Freedman's *Joe Louis: The Life of a Heavyweight*.

We found the story of Jackie Robinson in Fort Riley,

Kansas, in Ronald V. Dellums's article, "Jack all seasons," in the *New York Amsterdam New* 1987; and Joe Louis's article (as told to Meyer Barney Nagler), "Life Story of Joe Louis: He Crow in the Army," in the *New York Times*, No 1948.

The story about Joe and Sugar Ray Robinso Sibert was covered by a number of journals. on Dave Anderson's "A Corporal For Arlingt *New York Times*, April 20, 1981. We also pick quote "I'm a soldier like any other America from that article.

We found Joe's quote about loving Chap second installment of Joe's story in *Life* mag vember 15, 1948; and in *Joe Louis: My Life.*

Max talked about his visit to Berlin at the war in his autobiography.

Hitler's death scene was taken from Mich; *After Hitler.*

We found Max's ring earnings of a million Red McQueen's article ("Sports' Greatest Gold in the *Honolulu Advertiser*, January 28, 1947.

John Lardner's words about "the position Schmeling" were syndicated across the count North American Newspaper Alliance. We foun the *Arizona Daily Star*, July 12, 1945.

The story of Joe parting ways with Roxbor

lack is from PBS's *American Experience* online article ntitled "John Roxborough and Julian Black."

Joe's quote about the end of his second marriage to Marva is from his 1978 autobiography.

hapter 10

Ne found Joe's ring earnings ("more than $4 million dollars") in Bill Livingston's column, "The knockout," in the *Philadelphia Inquirer*, April 13, 1981.

The part about Joe's losing investments came from Chris Mead's *Joe Louis: Black Champion in White America*. Joe's paying of Vunies's tuition is from Thomas R. Hietala's *Fight of the Century*. We picked up Joe's quote about the tax expert talking Greek from his 1978 autobiography.

Wendell Smith's quote about Joe's restaurant bills appeared in his column in the *Pittsburgh Courier*, August 11, 1956.

We re-created the Marciano fight by consulting films of the fight. Joe's quote about being unable to duck Marciano's right hand was reported by the Associated Press, October 27, 1951.

Joe's troubles with the IRS were taken from Dave Anderson's article, "A Corporal For Arlington," in the *New York Times* of April 20, 1981.

Joe's quote about the tax situation was taken from his 1978 autobiography.

The scenes of Joe performing in Las Vegas are from

his 1978 autobiography. The information about his wrestling stint is from "Joe Louis's Heart Injury May End Wrestling Career" in the *St. Louis Post-Dispatch*, July 24, 1956.

Max's meeting with Jim Farley and the resulting deal with Coca-Cola were reported by Fritz Speiss of the Associated Press, June 24, 1973.

We researched Joe's appearance on *This Is Your Life* by watching films of the show, which originally aired October 23, 1960.

Epilogue

The scene at Caesars Palace ("A Night with the Champ") was taken from Shirley Eder's "Joe Louis Gets a Heavyweight Vegas Tribute" in the *Detroit Free Press* of November 12, 1978.

Martha Jefferson's deal with the government is from Lee Groves's "The Ring Celebrates the 100th Anniversary of Joe Louis' Birth." (TheRing.com, May 13, 2014.)

Joe's battle with cocaine, and his paranoid delusions, was reported by Dave Anderson of the *New York Times*, June 3, 1972. Joe's quote ("I guess I been around this stuff a long time . . .") was also found in this article.

Jesse Jackson's eulogy is from Dave Kindred, "A Sad Funeral for 'Poor Joe' Ends as Celebration of a Hero," *Washington Post*, April 18, 1981.

President Ronald Reagan's waiving of the eligibility

rules at Arlington National Cemetery can be found in the *Los Angeles Times* of April 16, 1981. "Burial of Joe Louis in Arlington OKd by Reagan."

Max's reason for staying in Nazi Germany during the war is from Fritz Spiess of the Associated Press, June 24, 1973.

BIBLIOGRAPHY

Books

Angelou, Maya. *I Know Why the Caged Bird Sings*. New York: Random House, 2002.

Astor, Gerald. *". . . And a Credit to His Race": The Hard Life and Times of Joseph Louis Barrow, a.k.a. Joe Louis*. New York: Saturday Review Press, 1974.

Bak, Richard. *Joe Louis: The Great Black Hope*. Boston: Da Capo Press, 1998.

Bass, Amy, ed. *In the Game: Race, Identity, and Sports in the Twentieth Century*. New York: Palgrave Macmillan, 2005.

DuBois, W. E. B. *The Souls of Black Folk*. New York: Modern Library, 2003.

Early, Gerald, ed. *The Culture of Bruising: Essays on Prizefighting, Literature, and Modern American Culture*. Hopewell, NJ: Ecco Press, 1994.

Edwards, John Carver. *Berlin Calling: American Broadcasters in Service to the Third Reich*. New York: Praeger, 1991.

Erenberg, Lewis A. *The Greatest Fight of Our Generation: Louis vs. Schmeling*. New York: Oxford University Press, 2006.

Freedman, Lew. *Joe Louis: The Life of a Heavyweight*. Jefferson, NC: McFarland, 2013.

Gibson, Truman K., Jr. *Knocking Down Barriers: My Fight*

for Black America. With Steve Huntley. Evanston, IL: Northwestern University Press, 2005.

Gitlin, Martin. *Powerful Moments in Sports: The Most Significant Sporting Events in American History.* Lanham, MD: Rowman & Littlefield, 2017.

Hietala, Thomas R. *The Fight of the Century: Jack Johnson, Joe Louis, and the Struggle for Racial Equality.* Armonk, NY: M. E. Sharpe, 2002.

Hughes, Langston. *The Collected Works of Langston Hughes.* Columbia: University of Missouri Press, 2001.

Jensen, Erik N. *Body by Weimar: Athletes, Gender, and German Modernity.* Oxford: Oxford University Press, 2010.

Jones, Michael. *After Hitler: The Last Ten Days of World War II in Europe.* New York: NAL Caliber, 2015.

Large, David Clay. *Nazi Games: The Olympics of 1936.* New York: W. W. Norton, 2007.

Lipsyte, Robert. *Joe Louis: A Champ for All America.* New York: HarperCollins, 1994.

Litwack, Leon F. *Trouble in Mind: Black Southerners in the Age of Jim Crow.* New York: Knopf, 1998.

Louis, Joe. *Joe Louis: My Life.* With Edna Rust and Art Rust Jr. New York: Harcourt Brace Jovanovich, 1978.

———. *My Life Story.* With Chester L. Washington and Haskell Cohen. New York: Duell, Sloan and Pearce, 1947.

Mandell, Richard D. *The Nazi Olympics.* Urbana: University of Illinois Press, 1987.

Margolick, David. *Beyond Glory: Joe Louis vs. Max Schmeling, and a World on the Brink.* New York: Knopf, 2005.

Marks, Carole. *Farewell—We're Good and Gone: The Great Black Migration.* Bloomington: Indiana University Press, 1989.

Mayer, Milton. *They Thought They Were Free: The Germans, 1933–45.* Chicago: University of Chicago Press, 2017.

Mead, Chris. *Joe Louis: Black Champion in White America.* Mineola, NY: Dover, 2010.

Miller, Patrick B., and David K. Wiggins, eds. *Sport and the Color Line: Black Athletes and Race Relations in Twentieth Century America.* New York: Routledge, 2004.

Monninger, Joseph. *Two Ton: One Fight, One Night; Tony Galento v. Joe Louis.* Hanover, NH: Steerforth Press, 2006.

Myler, Patrick. *Ring of Hate: Joe Louis vs. Max Schmeling; The Fight of the Century.* New York: Arcade, 2005.

Pfeifer, David. *Max Schmeling: Berufsboxer, Propagandafigur, Unternehmer.* Frankfurt: Campus Verlag, 2005.

Roberts, Randy. *Jack Dempsey: The Manassa Mauler.* Urbana: University of Illinois Press, 2003.

———. *Joe Louis: Hard Times Man.* New Haven, CT: Yale University Press, 2010.

———. *Papa Jack: Jack Johnson and the Era of White Hopes.* New York: Free Press, 1983.

Sacks, Marcy S. *Joe Louis: Sports and Race in Twentieth-Century America*. New York: Routledge, 2018.

Sammons, Jeffrey T. *Beyond the Ring: The Role of Boxing in American Society*. Urbana: University of Illinois Press, 1988.

Schapp, Jeremy. *Cinderella Man: James J. Braddock, Max Baer, and the Greatest Upset in Boxing History*. New York: Houghton Mifflin Harcourt, 2005.

———. *Triumph: The Untold Story of Jesse Owens and Hitler's Olympics*. New York: Houghton Mifflin, 2007.

Schmeling, Max. *Max Schmeling: An Autobiography*. Translated and edited by George B. von der Lippe. Chicago: Bonus Books, 1998.

Shirer, William L. *The Rise and Fall of the Third Reich: A History of Nazi Germany*. New York: Simon and Schuster, 1960.

Silber, Irwin. *Press Box Red: The Story of Lester Rodney, the Communist Who Helped Break the Color Line in American Sports*. Philadelphia: Temple University Press, 2003.

Silver, Mike. *Stars in the Ring: Jewish Champions in the Golden Age of Boxing*. Guilford, CT: Lyons Press, 2016.

Tygiel, Jules. *Baseball's Great Experiment: Jackie Robinson and His Legacy*. New York: Oxford University Press, 1997.

Washington, Booker T. *The Future of the American Negro*. New York: Negro Universities Press, 1969.

Wyman, David S. *The Abandonment of the Jews: America and the Holocaust, 1941–1945*. New York: Pantheon Books, 1984.

Magazines

Deford, Frank. "Almost a Hero." With Anita Verschoth. *Sports Illustrated*, Dec. 3, 2001.

Farrell, James T. "The Fall of Joe Louis." *Nation*, June 27, 1936.

Louis, Joe. "My Story—Joe Louis." With Meyer Berger and Barney Nagler. *Life*, Nov. 8, 1948.

———. "Part 2 of Joe Louis' Story." With Meyer Berger and Barney Nagler. *Life*, Nov. 15, 1948.

New Yorker. "Quick Thinker." Talk of the Town. June 13, 1936.

Robinson, Louie. "Joe Louis at 60." *Ebony*, Oct. 1973.

Sammons, Jeffrey T. "Boxing as a Reflection of Society: The Southern Reaction to Joe Louis." *The Journal of Popular Culture*, Spring 1983.

Newspapers

Abramson, Jesse. "Gathering Multitude Stops Traffic Near Stadium." *New York Herald Tribune*, June 23, 1938.

Adams, Caswell. "Joe Jacobs Says 1,000 Germans Coming to Schmeling-Louis Bout." *New York Herald Tribune*, April 29, 1938.

———. "Louis-Schmeling Bout to Draw 80,000 to Yankee Stadium Tonight." *New York Herald Tribune*, June 22, 1938.

Anderson, Dave. "A Corporal For Arlington." *New York Times*, April 20, 1981.

———. "Drugs and Demons for Joe Louis." *New York Times*, June 3, 1972.

Anderson, Margaret. "Schmeling Lost Ring Cash but His Wife Drips Mink." *Boston Globe*, March 4, 1962.

Associated Negro Press. "Grantland Rice Rates Joe Louis Next to Champion Max Baer." *Pittsburgh Courier*, May 4, 1935.

Associated Press. "'Ah'm Sho' Nuff Champeen Now,' Says Bomber Louis." *Marshfield (WI) News-Herald*, June 23, 1938.

———. "All Germany Thunderstruck over Defeat of Schmeling." *Cincinnati Enquirer*, June 23, 1938.

———. "And Is Harlem Happy?" *Cincinnati Enquirer*, June 23, 1938.

———. "Fighters' Statements Just Before Battle." *Atlanta Constitution*, June 22, 1938.

———. "Germany Acclaims Schmeling as National Hero for His Victory over Louis." *New York Times*. June 20, 1936.

———. "Goebbels Hails Victor." *New York Times*. June 20, 1936.

———. "Hitler Is Happy, Sends Greetings to Max Schmeling." *Evening News* (Wilkes-Barre, PA), June 20, 1936.

———. "Hitler Makes Triumphant Entry into Austria After Nazi Coup." *Salisbury (MD) Times*, March 12, 1938.

———. "Jacobs Will Not Name Louis-Schmeling Site Until After Maxie Fights Dudas." *Hartford (CT) Daily Courant*, April 3, 1938.

———. "Louis Seems Due to Get Hit." *Decatur (IL) Herald*, June 9, 1936.

———. "Max Sorry to Win over Lith on Foul." *Philadelphia Inquirer*, June 13, 1930.

———. "Saw Punch, but Couldn't Do Anything." *Boston Globe*, Oct. 27, 1951.

———. "Swing Music, the Susie-Q and Big Apple 'Take Over' After Bomber's Quick Victory." *Battle Creek (MI) Enquirer and Evening News*, June 23, 1938.

Atlanta Daily World. "Harlem Goes Wild." June 26, 1938.

Bacon, John U. "A Knockout Era: First Title for Louis Began Incredible Streak as Champ." *Detroit News and Free Press*, June 22, 1997.

Benson, Ted. "'The Battle of the Century—Joe Louis vs. Jim-Crow.'" Reprinted from *Sunday Worker*. *Pittsburgh Courier*, February 29, 1936.

Boston Globe. "Schmeling Penniless Wanderer in Germany Only Few Years Ago." July 4, 1931.

Boyack, James Edmund. "Psychological Superiority Will Beat Joe—Schmeling." *Pittsburgh Courier*, May 21, 1938.

Boyle, Havey J. "Sharkey Victor Over Schmeling, Wins Heavy Title." *Pittsburgh Post-Gazette*, June 22, 1932.

Brietz, Eddie. "'Black' Outlook in Louis' Camp Ballyhoo Paint." *Journal-Every Evening* (Wilmington, DE), June 10, 1936.

Chicago Daily Tribune. "Louis' Fists Claim 27th Victim." Jan. 19, 1936.

———. "Louis' Punches Stop Kracken in First Round." July 5, 1934.

———. "Round by Round Story of Louis-Schmeling Fight." June 20, 1936.

———. "Succession of K. O. Victories Mark Speedy Rise of Louis." June 26, 1935.

Chicago Defender. "Joe's Tax More Than Earnings." Jan. 28, 1957.

———. "Other Papers Say: A Negro Fighter." June 18, 1938.

Cunningham, Bill. "Schmeling's Fortune Vanishes with Collapse of German Arms." *Pittsburgh Post-Gazette*, July 18, 1945.

———. "Wartime Rumors Are Cleared Up by Max Schmeling." *Pittsburgh Post-Gazette*, July 17, 1945.

Dawson, James P. "11,000 See Louis Knock out Simms in First for Quickest Victory of Career." *New York Times*, Dec. 15, 1936.

———. "Schmeling Winner on Sharkey's Foul; 80,000 at Title Bout." *New York Times*, June 13, 1930.

———. "70,000 See Sharkey Outpoint Schmeling to Win World Title." *New York Times*, June 22, 1932.

Dixon, Randy. "How Will Joe Fare Against Max Schmeling?" *Philadelphia Tribune*, March 3, 1938.

Dunkley, Charles. "Schmeling Rose to Fame from Penniless Wanderer," *Minneapolis Tribune*, July 6, 1931.

Evans, Orrin C. "Harlem Hits the Top and 'Blows Lid Off' After Louis Victory." *Philadelphia Tribune*, June 23, 1938.

Gould, Alan. "Long Wait for Title Bout Costs Schmeling $100,000." *San Bernardino Daily Sun* (California), Sept. 5, 1937.

Grayson, Harry. "Challenger Schmeling Lets Louis

Worry About the Outcome of Second Meeting." *Muncie (IN) Evening Press*, June 13, 1938.

Greene, Roger. "How Can Brown Bomber Pay Up $2,350,000?" *State Journal* (Lansing, MI), March 10 1957.

Greenville News (Greenville, SC). "Race Riots Break Out over Country." July 5, 1910.

Harris, Ed. "Joe Louis to Take Max in Fourth Round." *Philadelphia Tribune*, June 18, 1936.

International News Service. "Louis Feasts on Ice Cream After Battle." *Evening News* (Wilkes-Barre, PA), June 23, 1938.

———. "Max Schmeling No Drawing Card." *Corsicana (TX) Daily Sun*, May 20, 1954.

Jackson, Kent. "Jews Pray for Louis Victory on Eve of Heavyweight Battle." *Philadelphia Tribune*, June 23, 1938.

James, Edwin L. "Hitler Is Victor Again as Nazis Grab Austria." *New York Times*, March 13, 1938.

Jarrett, Vernon. "What Joe Louis Gave to Us." *Chicago Tribune*, April 15, 1981.

Johnson, Jack. "'Dempsey Was World's Most Overrated Champion'—Johnson." *Pittsburgh Courier*, April 20, 1929.

———. "Langford Could Have Easily Whipped Dempsey—Johnson." *Pittsburgh Courier*, April 27, 1929.

Jones, Lucius. "Joe Louis and Schmeling Tell How They Will Beat Each Other in Interesting Articles." *Atlanta Daily World*, June 18, 1938.

Jones, William. "Nazis Aid Max." *Afro-American* (Baltimore), June 25, 1938.

Jordan, John. "Nazis Threaten Louis: Champ Guarded Heavily." *Journal and Guide* (Norfolk, VA), June 25, 1938.

Journal and Guide (Norfolk, VA). "Champion Rough on Spar Mates." June 18, 1938.

———. "Marva and Joe Have 'Family Bet' on Knockout in Three Rounds." June 25, 1938.

Keefe, Wm. McG. "German's Courage Big Factor in Victory." *Times-Picayune* (New Orleans), June 20, 1936.

Kessler, Gene. "Schmeling Studied Movies of Dempsey." *Boston Globe,* June 14, 1938.

Kieran, John. "In the Wake of Schmeling's Night Out." *New York Times,* Jan. 24, 1938.

Kirksey, George. "Joe Louis Turns in Disappointing Workout." *Wisconsin State Journal* (Madison), May 25, 1936.

———. "Louis Whips Paulino by Technical Knockout After Basque Hits Mat." *Sunday Herald* (Provo, UT), Dec. 15, 1935.

Lardner, John. "Schmeling's Record After Crete Will Bear Scrutiny." *Arizona Daily Star* (Tucson), July 12, 1945.

Laufer, Werner. "Elevator Man First Victim of Max," pt. 2 of "The Life Story of Max Schmeling." *Arizona Daily Star* (Tuscon), June 20, 1930.

Lear, John. "5,000,000 Jews Facing New Exodus." *Washington Post,* Feb. 28, 1937.

Lewis, Perry. "Jack Great Fighter from His Neck Down." *Philadelphia Inquirer*, June 14, 1930.

———. "Schmeling Fouled, Wins Championship Bout with Sharkey." *Philadelphia Inquirer*, June 13, 1930.

———. "Sharkey Beats Schmeling And Takes Crown." *Philadelphia Inquirer*, June 22, 1932.

MacGowan, Gault. "Der Max Plans for New Role." *Muncie (IN) Star*, June 30, 1945.

Manchester Guardian (UK). "German Boxer's Success." June 26, 1936.

Margolick, David. "'Save Me, Joe Louis!'" *Los Angeles Times*, Nov. 7, 2005.

McCormick, Bill. "A Champion's Most Feared Foe." *Daily Times* (New Philadelphia, OH), Jan. 14, 1961.

McLemore, Henry. "New York Goes Nuts over Louis-Schmeling Fight," *Amarillo (TX) Globe*, June 21, 1938.

———. "Fight Natural Looms in Louis-Schmeling Bout." *Chester Times* (Chester, PA), June 22, 1938.

———. "They Can't Find Enough Sparring Pards to Meet Joe Louis' Needs," *Wisconsin State Journal* (Madison), May 27, 1936.

Monroe, Al. "Louis Beats Schmeling." *Chicago Defender*, June 25, 1938.

Montgomery, Paul. "Schmeling Still Battles to Grasp the Past." *New York Times*, June 19, 1988.

New York Amsterdam News. "Bomber Tossing Vicious Punches: Spar Mate Sorry for Max Schmeling." June 11, 1938.

———. "Harlem Paces the Nation Celebrating Victory by Joe Louis over Schmeling." July 2, 1938.

———. "Harlem Tense as Bout Nears." June 18, 1938.

———. "Louis Starts Gunning for Max." April 9, 1938.

New York Herald Tribune. "Overcast Sky Gives Jacobs Early Worries." June 23, 1938.

New York Times. "Harlem Disorders Mark Louis Defeat." June 20, 1936.

———. "Schmeling Guest of Hitler at Lunch." June 28, 1936.

Nunn, William G. "Brown Bomber Kayoes Sharkey in Thrilling Bout." *Pittsburgh Courier*, Aug. 22, 1936.

———. "Daily Routine at Joe Louis' Ideal Camp Revealed." *Pittsburgh Courier*, June 8, 1935.

O'Boyle, Thomas F. "Louis-Schmeling Fight, 50 Years Ago, Made Propaganda, Lifelong Friendship." *Wall Street Journal*, June 19, 1986.

Padwe, Sandy. "Joe Louis: Sleek, Powerful, Alert . . . 'Whoever Dreamed It'd Come to This?'" *Detroit Free Press*, June 14, 1970.

Pegler, Westbrook. "Joe Louis Is the New Champion of the World, but That's Where the Trouble Starts." *Washington Post*, June 23, 1937.

———. "Sharkey Wins Decision; He's Ring Champion." *Chicago Daily Tribune*, June 22, 1932.

———. "Why Be Upset About Robbery of Schmeling?" *Chicago Daily Tribune*, June 23, 1932.

Pelham, Robert A. "Brown Bomber Has 'Happy Family' at Camp." *Atlanta Daily World*, June 4, 1936.

Philadelphia Tribune. "Record Crowd Raves as Louis Biffs Spar Mates." June 16, 1938.

———. "Ticket Sale Underway for Joe Louis–Max Schmeling Fite." June 2, 1938.

Pittsburgh Courier. "Town Where Joe Louis First Saw Light of Day Takes Victory Calmly." July 2, 1938.

Ratcliffe, Robert M. "Schmeling Defeat in 1st Round After Hitting Canvas Third Time." *Atlanta Daily World,* June 23, 1938.

Rice, Grantland. "Schmeling Explodes 'Myth of Superman' with Kayo Win over Louis." *Los Angeles Times,* June 20, 1936.

Ross, Albion. "Big Crowds Assured for Berlin Olympics." *New York Times,* Dec. 15, 1935.

———. "Schmeling, Home, Hailed by Reich." *New York Times,* June 27, 1936.

Runyon, Damon. "Many Critics And Spectators Agree With Max's Pilot." *Pittsburgh Post-Gazette,* June 22, 1932.

Salt Lake Tribune. "Jack Johnson Still Champion." July 5, 1910.

Schmeling, Max. "German Heavy Fond of Good Books; Paints." *Montana Standard* (Butte), Feb. 12, 1929.

———. "Knockout by Unknown Gave Max Setback." *Montana Standard* (Butte), Feb. 19, 1929.

———. "Max Nervous Youth Night of Risko Mix." *Montana Standard* (Butte), Feb. 23, 1929.

———. "'Joe Louis Won't Tag Me Like That'—Schmeling." *Pittsburgh Post-Gazette,* Dec. 14, 1935.

———. "Max Schmeling at Home." *Montana Standard* (Butte), Sept. 8, 1929.

——. "Schmeling in Strong Man's Role in Show." *Montana Standard* (Butte), Feb. 13, 1929.

Sharkey, Jack. "Jack Happy, Pays Tribute To Schmeling." *Pittsburgh Post-Gazette*, June 22, 1932.

Smith, Wendell. "The Tragic Saga of Joe Louis . . . Fighter." *Pittsburgh Courier*, Aug. 11, 1956.

——. "You Can't Forget Can He?" Smitty's Sport Spurts. *Pittsburgh Courier*, June 18, 1938.

Smith, Wilfrid. "Joe Louis Looks like That Tonic Boxing Needed." *Chicago Sunday Tribune*, July 21, 1935.

——. "Schmeling Faces Long Stay in Hospital." *Chicago Daily Tribune*, June 24, 1938.

——. "Schmeling Whips Joe Louis." *Chicago Daily Tribune*, June 20, 1936.

Snider, Steve. "Louis Awaits Schmeling After Thomas Is Kayoed." *Dayton (OH) Herald*, April 2, 1938.

Spiess, Fritz. "Schmeling Prosperous Businessman." *Sunday Telegram* (Elmira, NY), June 24, 1973.

The Globe and Mail (Toronto). "Huge Stadium Fills with Avid Fight Fans." June 26, 1938.

United Press. "Austria Opens Anti-Semitic Campaign." *Los Angeles Times*, Feb. 19, 1938.

——. "Hitler Sends Greetings to German Boxer." *Ogden (UT) Standard-Examiner*, June 20, 1936.

Universal Service. "Quiet Reception for Max in Germany." *Pittsburgh Post-Gazette*, July 5, 1930.

Van Ness, Fred. "Schmeling Agrees to Fight for Jacobs." *New York Times*, June 5, 1936.

——. "Schmeling to Fight Louis in Sept." *New York Times*, June 29, 1935.

Ward, Arch. "Louis, Schmeling Fight for Title Tonight." *Chicago Daily Tribune*, June 22, 1938.

Washington, Chester. "Joe Louis Resolves to Beat Schmeling." *Pittsburgh Courier*, Jan. 8, 1938.

———. "Louis Starts Drill Siege in Pompton Camp." *Pittsburgh Courier*, June 4, 1938.

———. "Visiting the Joe Louis Training Camp." Sez Ches. *Pittsburgh Courier*, June 8 1935.

Washington, Chester, and William G. Nunn. "The Life Story of Joe Louis." *Pittsburgh Courier*, May 4, 1935.

Weber, Harry B. "Max Will Kayo Joe in Ten, Says Joe Jacobs." *Afro-American* (Baltimore), March 26, 1938.

White, Al. "25,000 Drawn to Harlem by Our Joe." *Journal and Guide* (Norfolk, VA), June 25, 1938.

Williams, Joe. "You're Next, Maxie!" *Pittsburgh Press, December 14, 1935.*

———. "Louis Isn't The Same Man He Was—But He's The Same Fighter." *Pittsburgh Press*, June 16, 1936.

Young, Fay. "Past—Present—Future." *Chicago Defender*, April 16, 1938.

Films, Television, and Radio

"The Fight." Written, directed, and produced by Barak Goodman. *American Experience*, PBS, Oct. 18, 2004.

Joe Louis: America's Hero Betrayed. Written by Ouisie Shapiro. HBO, 2008.

"The Joe Louis–Max Schmeling Boxing Match," June 22,

1938. In "The Fight of the Century: Louis vs. Schmeling." National Public Radio, Nov. 25, 2006, www.npr.org/player/embed/6515548/6518647.

The Rise and Fall of Jim Crow. Directed by Richard Wormser and Bill Jersey. PBS, October 2002.

The Sweet Science: Shadow Boxing; The Journey of the African-American Boxer. ESPN Classic, 1999.

PHOTO CREDITS

and Photographs Division; **86**: Scherl/Sueddeutsche Zeitung Photo/Alamy Stock Photo; **89**: Bettmann/Getty Images; **94**: Bettmann/Getty Images; **98**: Scherl/ Sueddeutsche Zeitung Photo/Alamy Stock Photo; **101**: SuperStock/Alamy Stock Photo; **110**: Associated Press; **114**: Everett Collection Historical/Alamy Stock Photo; **120**: Pictorial Press Ltd/Alamy Stock Photo; **123**: Associated Press/Library of Congress Prints and Photographs Division; **126**: Unidentified artist for Graphics Division/Office of Facts and Figures, 1942/ National Portrait Gallery, Smithsonian Institution; **128**: Detroit Historical Society; **131**: Library of Congress Prints and Photographs Division; **137**: Everett Collection Historical/Alamy Stock Photo; **138**: Everett Collection Historical/Alamy Stock Photo; **140**: Associated Press; **148**: PA Images/Alamy Stock Photo

INDEX